MC

Ele

By

T. SCOTT GILLIGAN, J.D.
and
THOMAS F.H. STUEVE, A.B., L.L.B., A.M.

Published 1940

Revised 1946

Revised 1956

Reprinted 1960

Revised 1963

Revised 1966

Reprinted 1968

Reprinted 1971

Reprinted 1973

Revised 1975

Revised 1980

Reprinted 1982

Revised 1984

Revised 1988

Rewritten 1995

Revised 2003

Revised 2011

Published by The Cincinnati Foundation for Mortuary Education
645 North Bend Road
Cincinnati, Ohio 45224

ISBN 1-883031-02-8

To: Frank J. Gilligan

PREFACE TO ELEVENTH
REVISED EDITION

The rapid pace of change and developments in the laws that govern the funeral profession and the death care industry necessitate yet another update of Mortuary Law. Congress and federal regulators have instituted new privacy laws, modified the ADA, updated wage & hour regulations, and changed the tax code in several ways that impact funeral homes. State egislature have also played an important part by enacting or amending right of disposition statutes, increasing preneed and cremation regulations, and adopting regulatory schemes for new forms of disposition such as alkaline hydrolysis.

On the publication of this Eleventh Revision of this Mortuary Law, I would like to thank Karen Giles, the President of the Cincinnati College of Mortuary Science for the continuing opportunity to update Mortuary Law. I would also like to thank Patty Carter for her invaluable administrative assistance.

T. Scott Gilligan

Cincinnati, Ohio
December 1, 2011

TABLE OF CONTENTS

CHAPTER ONE: INTRODUCTION

1.1   Study of Mortuary Law 1

1.2   Sources of Mortuary Law 1

        a. State Laws and Regulations

        b. Case Law

        c. Common Law

        d. Federal Law

1.3   Obligations of Funeral Professional 3

CHAPTER TWO: DISPOSITION OF THE DEAD

2.1   Dead Body Defined 5

2.2   Legal Status of a Dead Body 5

2.3   Necessity of Disposition 6

2.4   Respect for the Deceased and Survivors... 7

2.5   Methods of Disposition 8

CHAPTER THREE: RIGHTS OF PARTIES UNDERTAKING DISPOSITION

3.1   In General... 11

3.2   Right of Custody... 11

3.3   Right to Control the Funeral 12

3.4   Right to Choose Disposition... 14

3.5   Funeral Director with Right of Disposition 14

3.6   Funeral Contract... 15

        a. In General

        b. Disclosures

        c. Contract Terminology

CHAPTER FOUR: WHO HAS THE RIGHT OF DISPOSITION

4.1   Introduction... 19

4.2   Right of Disposition Statutes 19

4.3   Mechanism to Control Disposition 19

4.4   Priority List 20

4.5   Forfeiture of Right of Disposition 20

        a. Missing Relatives

        b. Majority Control

        c. Waiver of Uncooperative Relatives

        d. Homicide Cases

4.6   Protection for Funeral Homes 21

4.7   Anatomical Gift Act.. 22

CHAPTER FIVE: DUTIES OF THE FUNERAL DIRECTOR

5.1 In General 25

5.2 Statutory Duties 25
    a. Permits
    b. Health Laws and Regulations

5.3 Contractual Obligations 26
    a. Negligent Embalming
    b. Negligent Funeral Directing
    c. Safeguard the Body
    d. Privacy
    e. Defective Merchandise
    f. Transportation
    g. Aftercare

5.4 Tort Liability 30
    a. Wrongfully Withholding a Body
    b. Loss of the Body
    c. Mutilation of the Body
    d. Injury to Invitees
    e. Injury to Pallbearers and Clergy

5.5 Mental Anguish... 34
    a. Physical Impact
    b. Intentional Infliction of Mental Distress
    c. Contractual Breaches
    d. Negligent Infliction of Mental Distress
    e. Punitive Damages

CHAPTER SIX: LIABILITY FOR FUNERAL EXPENSES

6.1 In General... 37

6.2 Liability of the Estate 37
    a. Primary Obligor
    b. Reasonableness of the Funeral Bill
    c. Collection Against an Estate

6.3 Liability for Funeral Expenses of Dependent 38

6.4 Contractual Liability 39

6.5 Liability of Executor or Administrator 40

6.6 Liability of State 40

CHAPTER SEVEN: CREMATION

7.1 Overview... 41

7.2 Authorization to Cremate 41

7.3 Other Cremation Forms 43

7.4 Investigating Third Party Crematories 43
    a. Crematory Records Request

b. *Interview of Crematory Management*
c. *Crematory Inspection*

CHAPTER EIGHT: DISINTERMENT

8.1 Disinterment Defined 47

8.2 Disinterment Disfavored 47

8.3 Disinterment in the Public Interest 47

8.4 Disinterment for Private Purposes 48

8.5 Unauthorized Disinterments 50

CHAPTER NINE: FUNERAL HOMES

9.1 Defined 51

9.2 Licensing and Regulation 51

9.3 Location of Funeral Homes 52
    a. *Nuisance*
    b. *Zoning Regulations*
    c. *Conclusion*

9.4 Licensing of Other Death Care Facilities 54

9.5 Americans with Disabilities Act 55
    a. *Overview*
    b. *Priorities*
    c. *Readily Achievable Test*
    d. *Withholding of Services*
    e. *Enforcement*

CHAPTER TEN: PRENEED FUNERAL CONTRACTS

10.1 In General 59

10.2 Preneed Funding by Trust 59

10.3 Preneed Funding by Insurance 61

10.4 Taxation of Preneed Income 62

10.5 Medicaid/SSI 62
    a. *Irrevocable Preneed Funeral Contracts*
    b. *Burial Space Exclusion*
    c. *Burial Funds Exclusion*

10.6 FTC Door-To-Door Regulation 64

CHAPTER ELEVEN: WAGE AND HOUR LAWS

11.1 Overview 67

11.2 Enforcement 67

11.3 Coverage Under the FLSA 67
    a. *Employers*
    b. *Employees*

11.4 2004 Update to DOL Regulations 69

11.5 Independent Contractors 71

11.6 Recordkeeping 71

11.7 Minimum Wage 71

11.8 Overtime Pay 71
        a. General Requirements
        b. Salaried Employees
        c. Variable Workweek Agreement

11.9 Equal Pay Act 73

11.10 Particular Wage and Hour Issues for Funeral Homes 73
        a. Caretaker
        b. On-Call Employees

CHAPTER TWELVE: FEDERAL EMPLOYMENT LAW

12.1 Introduction 77

12.2 Americans with Disabilities Act 77
        a. Overview
        b. Coverage of ADA
        c. Purpose of ADA
        d. Disability
        e. Americans With Disability Act Amendment Act
        f. Essential Functions
        g. Undue Hardship

12.3 Civil Rights Laws 81
        a. Overview
        b. Coverage of the Civil Rights Laws
        c. Scope of the Civil Rights Laws
        d. Enforcement

CHAPTER THIRTEEN: OCCUPATIONAL SAFETY AND HEALTH ACT

13.1 Overview 85

13.2 Enforcement 85

13.3 Notice and Recordkeeping 86

13.4 General Requirements Standard 86

13.5 Specific OSHA Standards Applicable to Funeral Homes 86

13.6 Formaldehyde Exposure Standard 87
        a. Overview
        b. Ongoing Compliance Responsibilities
        c. Remedial Measures
        d. Additional Remedial Steps

13.7 Hazard Communication Standard 89

13.8 Bloodborne Pathogen Standard 90

13.9   Needstick Safety and Prevention Act 91

CHAPTER FOURTEEN: FTC FUNERAL RULE

14.1   Introduction.. 93
14.2   General Price List... 93
        a. Introductory Matters
        b. Itemization of Sixteen Goods and Services
        c. Mandatory Disclosures
        d. Package Funerals
        e. Distribution of GPL

14.3   Casket Price List 98
        a. Introductory Matters
        b. Casket and Alternative Container Listings
        c. Distribution of Casket Price List

14.4   Outer Burial Container Price List 99
        a. Introductory Matters
        b. Outer Burial Container Listings
        c. Mandatory Disclosure
        d. Distribution of Outer Burial Container Price List

14.5   Statement of Funeral Goods and Services Selected.................... 100
        a. Itemization Entries
        b. Mandatory Disclosures
        c. Distribution of Statement

14.6   Telephone Price Disclosures 101
14.7   Misrepresentations 102
        a. Embalming
        b. Caskets for Direct Cremation
        c. Outer Burial Containers
        d. Legal and Cemetery Requirements
        e. Preservation and Protective Claims
        f. Cash Advance Items

14.8   Tying Arrangements 103
        a. Non-Declinable Basic Service Fee
        b. Legal Requirements
        c. Impossible, Impractical or Excessively Burdensome
        d. Third Party Merchandise

14.9   Prior Permission to Embalm.. 105
        a. State or Local Law
        b. Prior Permission to Embalm
        c. Exigent Circumstances

14.10 Retention of Price Documents 106
14.11 Enforcement 106

CHAPTER FIFTEEN: FEDERAL REGULATION OF FUNERAL BILLING AND COLLECTION

15.1   Introduction 115

15.2   Truth-in-Lending 115
   a. Coverage of the Act
   b. Definition of a Creditor
   c. Definition of Consumer Credit
   d. Definition of a Finance Charge
   e. Preneed Arrangements
   f. Advertising
   g. Refinancing and Extensions
   h. Required Disclosures
   i. Multiple Purchasers
   j. Disclosure Examples

15.3   Magnuson-Moss Warranty Act 121
   a. Disclaimer of Warranties
   b. Adoption of Manufacturers' Warranties
   c. Display of Manufacturers' Warranties

15.4   FTC Credit Practices Regulations 122
   a. Cognovit Note or Confession of Judgement
   b. Executory Waiver
   c. Assignment of Wages
   d. Security Interest in Household Goods
   e. Co-Signor Practices
   f. Late Charges

CHAPTER SIXTEEN: FEDERAL PRIVACY LAWS

16.1   In General 127

16.2   Gramm-Leach-Bliley Act 127

16.3   HIPAA 128

16.4   FTC/FCC Do-Not-Call Regulation 130

16.5   Fair Debt Collection Practices Act 131

MORTUARY LAW

Chapter One

INTRODUCTION

1.1 Study of Mortuary Law

To be successful in funeral service, both as a caregiver and as an entrepreneur, the funeral director must have a working knowledge of the many laws that impact the profession. This body of law, which is dynamic and growing, is defined for purposes of this book as "mortuary law" or "funeral law."

Funeral law consists of the rules and principles that society has established for the handling and disposition of the dead. It provides rights and places duties upon the survivors of the decedent so that the dead can be memorialized without jeopardizing the health and safety of the overall community. In so doing, that law also places upon funeral directors a detailed set of duties and obligations which they owe to the survivors of the decedent, the clients they contract with, their employees, and the community where the funeral home is located.

The purpose of this book is to give students sufficient knowledge of the substance and operation of funeral law so that they can fulfill their duties and obligations in a professional and ethical manner. The book will strive not to be simply a recital of statute and case laws, but more an explanation of what is required of the funeral director under the law.

1.2 Sources of Mortuary Law

Government regulation of business, especially the funeral profession, has greatly expanded in the past thirty-five years. The sources of that increasing regulatory scope are as follows:

a. State Laws and Regulations

The states are the principal regulators of the funeral profession. Each state has an inherent authority known as its police power. The police power empowers the state legislature to enact laws for the protection of the general welfare, health and safety. Included in this power is the authority to restrict individuals in the exercise of certain activities so as to promote the common good.

The police power of the state empowers it to set standards and requires licenses of individuals that wish to practice a certain profession or trade. Pursuant to this power, every state in the country except one (Colorado) licenses the funeral profession. Individuals seeking to hold themselves out to the public as funeral directors must achieve a certain educational level, undergo specialized training, and obtain licenses from the state. In order to retain the license, the funeral director must perform his or her duties in an ethical manner that conforms with the many governmental regulations which the state imposes.

Although state legislatures enact the licensing laws and other statutes that govern the funeral profession, typically the legislature will delegate to an administrative agency the task of the day-to-day regulation. Thus, most states have boards of funeral directors and embalmers that oversee the licensing statutes, investigate and inspect funeral homes, and conduct enforcement actions against those in the profession not in compliance with the laws. State boards usually have a number of funeral directors on the board as well as members of the public that represent consumer interests.

In carrying out their regulatory tasks, state boards often are given power by the legislature to promulgate administrative regulations. For example, the law may delegate to the state board the authority to designate what equipment a funeral home must have in order to receive a license. As long as the regulation promulgated by the board is within the delegation of power it has received from the legislature, the administrative regulation will generally be upheld by the courts.

b. Case Law

Many of the principles that govern funeral law have their roots in the decisions of state and local courts. A court interprets the law and applies it to the facts of the case it is deciding. Therefore, once a law is enacted, it is up to the court to decide precisely what the legislature intended by enacting the law. The court construes the scope and applicability of the law to the facts before it.

Courts are occasionally called upon to decide the constitutionality of a statute or regulation. The U.S. Constitution is the ultimate authority in the country. In addition, each state constitution is the primary law of the respective states. Therefore, if a statute violates a constitutional principle, it is struck down as unconstitutional. For example, in 2011 a federal district court found that Louisiana's law which required an individual to have a funeral director's license in order to sell caskets was an unconstitutional deprivation of due process. Similarly, if an administrative regulation exceeds the authority of the regulatory body promulgating it, it is declared void.

Once a particular issue is resolved by a court, a principle is established which will control future decisions by that court or lower courts. This is known as the doctrine of stare decisis. It means that a court deciding a point gives to precedent the authority of established law. Absent some other conditions or a changed attitude on the part of the court, the doctrine will be followed and the preceding decision will control the ruling in the new case.

In many states, it is the probate court that has the authority to settle controversies concerning dead bodies. The probate court is the court that generally controls the disposition of a decedent's estate and settles disputes over wills. Therefore, in most states, if a family were having a dispute regarding the final disposition of a body, they would apply to the probate court to determine the proper resolution of the dispute.

c. Common Law

Not all law is codified in statutes and regulations. There is a great body of unwritten law that is referred to as the "Common Law". The Common Law consists of maxims, principles, and judicial decisions that have been passed down from hundreds of years of jurisprudence. Much of the Common Law has its roots in English and early colonial law.

The Common Law fills up gaps in our legal system. It provides most of the principles that govern our basic rights as members of society. Therefore, it is not surprising that many aspects of funeral law are impacted by the Common Law. For example, the establishment of who is given the right to take possession of the body upon death and direct its ultimate disposition has its roots in the Common Law.

d. Federal Law

Prior to 1980, funeral law was generated primarily by state legislatures and judicial decisions by state and local courts. These sources, combined with the Common Law, govern nearly all aspects of the profession.

In the past thirty years, the federal government has emerged as a major source of regulation for the funeral director. Some regulations, such as the Federal Trade Commission's Funeral Rule, are specific to funeral service; other statutes and regulations, such as the safety requirements of the Occupational Safety and Health Administration or the Americans with Disabilities Act cover many businesses.

The fact that over one-third of this book is now devoted solely to federal laws and regulations demonstrates the growing importance to the funeral industry of the federal government.

1.3   Obligations of the Funeral Professional

In the past thirty-five years, the funeral director has come under a dizzying array of government regulations. Not surprisingly, this has placed the funeral director under even greater pressure in carrying out his or her duties. The funeral directors who will be successful are those that see government regulation for what it is – a well-intended but often imperfect method to protect consumers and employees. Funeral directors who make a whole-hearted attempt to understand the laws and regulations and incorporate them into the funeral home business routine will often find means to soften the disruption caused by the regulation while improving upon its beneficial effects. For example, some funeral directors have reported that, in implementing the OSHA regulations discussed in Chapter Thirteen, they have taken steps beyond those required by the OSHA regulations to improve the safety of employees who work in the preparation room.

Implementations of the Americans with Disabilities Act standards (see Chapters Nine and Twelve) will undoubtedly cause some funeral directors, especially those in older buildings, to undertake expensive capital improvements. However, the elderly and disabled who arrange or attend funeral services in those facilities will greatly appreciate the funeral director's concern for their comfort. Although such benefits are intangible, funeral directors are well aware that a successful funeral operation is the direct result of the accumulation over the years of intangibles such as goodwill and trust. Families, even those that do not benefit directly from wheelchair ramps and accessible bathrooms, will take recognition of the funeral home's consideration for the disabled.

As is often heard these days, putting up with government regulation is one of the costs of doing business. However, the resourceful funeral director does not look upon government regulation as a burdensome cost. Rather, to him or her it is a challenge that, if understood and accepted, can be a tool for improving service to families while protecting the health and safety of funeral home employees and the public.

Chapter Two

DISPOSITION OF THE DEAD

2.1 Dead Body Defined

The term "dead body" means specifically the body of a human being deprived of life but not yet entirely disintegrated. The term "corpse" is a synonymous term with the term "dead body". A body to be legally a dead body or corpse must meet three conditions. It must be the body of a human being, without life, and not entirely disintegrated.

Given the advancements in technology in the past 50 years, society's definition of "death" is in flux. In the 1950 case of *Thomas v. Anderson*, 96 Cal. App. 2d 371, 215 P. 2d 478, the court stated that death occurs when life ceases, which takes place when the heart stops beating and respiration ends. In the 1979 case of *Lovats v. District Court*, 198 Col. 419, 601 P. 2d 1072, the court stated that for legal and medical purposes, an individual who has sustained irreversible cessation of all functioning of the brain, including the brain stem, is dead. With modern medical technology, this latter definition is becoming the most widely used, because a person's heart or lungs may continue to function through artificial means even though the person has no brain function.

Under the law, a dead body is a body that has not yet disintegrated. Therefore, the remains of a cremated body, a disintegrated corpse or the bones of a skeleton do not constitute a "dead body" in the eyes of the law. In *State v. Glass*, 27 O. App. 2d 214, 273 N.E. 2d 893, a real estate developer who had ordered bulldozers to level land upon which an old cemetery was located was charged with a violation of Ohio's "Grave Robbery" statute. The site that was developed contained the graves of three persons buried about 120 years earlier. In reversing the conviction of the developer, the Appeals Court stated as follows:

> "A cadaver is not an everlasting thing. After undergoing an undefined degree of decomposition, it ceases to be a dead body in the eyes of the law."

2.2 Legal Status of a Dead Body

For over one thousand years, the courts have struggled over whether a dead body does or does not constitute property. In early English law, it was established that the dead body was within the exclusive control of the Church. From this notion, courts developed the principle that no individual had property rights in the dead body. Thus, it was said that a dead body is the property of no one and there is no property in a dead body.

As the law became more secular, courts began to acknowledge that the surviving spouse and next of kin do have a right to take possession of the body to arrange its disposition. While they stopped short of declaring that a dead body was the "property" of the surviving family member, they recognized that survivors had quasi-property rights in the dead body.

One of the more scholarly analyses of this quasi-property right is found in the decision of the U.S. Sixth Circuit Court of Appeals in *Brotherton v. Cleveland*, 923 F.2d 477 (6th Cir. 1991). In that case, a surviving spouse sued the county coroner for removing her deceased husband's corneas without her consent. The court was faced with the issue of whether the spouse had been deprived of property without the due process of law.

The coroner's office maintained that the dead body was not property, and therefore, the spouse had no property rights to the corneas. The Court of Appeals refused to adopt the coroner's narrow interpretation. Rather, it analyzed exactly what "property" is:

> "The concept of 'property' in the law is extremely broad and abstract. The legal definition of 'property' most often refers not to a particular physical object, but rather to the legal bundle of rights recognized in that object. Thus, 'property' is often conceptualized as a 'bundle of rights.' The 'bundle of rights' which have been associated with property include the right to possess, to use, to exclude, to profit, and to dispose."

Finding that American courts had rejected early English law and had recognized that the next of kin has a quasi-property right in the decedent's body for the purpose of disposition, the court held that the spouse had a possessory right to the body and that the coroner's taking of the corneas violated that right.

The court's decision in *Brotherton* is consistent with the prevailing view of the dead body as "quasi-property." It is not property in the commercial sense, but the law does provide a bundle of rights to the next of kin in relation to that body. The survivor is given the right to take the body for purposes of disposition, to allow body parts to be used within the confines of the law, to exclude others from possession of the body, and to dispose of the body. This bundle of rights renders the dead body the quasi-property of the person holding the right of disposition.

2.3 Necessity of Disposition

It is well within the police powers of the government to require the orderly disposition of the dead in order to promote public health. Society has recognized that health and safety concerns, as well as public morality, necessitate the disposition of the dead by regulated methods. Courts have regularly upheld criminal statutes requiring the proper disposition of the dead. In State v. Robbinson, 202 Neb. 210, 274 N.E. 2d 553 (1979), an individual had placed a dead body in the trunk of a car and then abandoned the automobile. He was convicted under a Nebraska statute making it a criminal offense for any person to throw away or abandon any dead human body, or any portion thereof, in any place other than a regular place for burial and under properly issued death certificates. The Nebraska Supreme Court upheld the constitutionality of the criminal statute.

Statutes which impose criminal penalties for the failure to bury or incinerate a corpse within a reasonable time after death have been applied to funeral directors. In two New York cases, (*People ex rel. Travis v. Daniels* 57 NYS 2d 457 (1945); *People v. Ackley* 62 NYS 2d 771 (1946)), funeral directors who had accepted bodies but failed to see to their proper disposition were held to be criminally liable.

In the wake of the Tri-State Crematory scandal that arose in Noble, Georgia in 2002, where a crematory operator discarded over 300 bodies rather than cremating them, a number of states adopted new laws or strengthened existing criminal laws on abandoning dead bodies. Georgia, for example, now provides that any one who throws away or abandons a dead human body or portion thereof is guilty of a felony punishable by one to three years in jail.

2.4 Respect for the Deceased and Survivors

In addition to public health and safety concerns, courts have also recognized that the states have a valid interest in protecting survivors and insuring them sufficient privacy to carry out the disposition of their deceased family members in a respectful manner. In *National Archives and Records Administration v. Favish*, 541 U.S. 157 (2004), the U.S. Supreme Court held that, in respect to an individual's request, death scene photographs of a public official were protected from disclosure under an exemption to the Freedom of Information Act. The Court based its holdings on cultural traditions and common law protections. The Court noted the respect that civilizations have provided to burial rights and their counterparts. The Court then acknowledged the "well-established cultural tradition acknowledging a family's control over the body and death images of the deceased," as well as a survivor's right of privacy in protecting the memory of the deceased.

A similar holding was provided in *Phelps-Roper v. Strickland*, 539 F.3rd 356 (2008), when the Sixth Circuit upheld an Ohio law which prohibited protests within 300 feet of a funeral or burial service. Against claims that the law violated the free speech guarantees of the First Amendment, the Court held that "burial rites implicate the most basic and universal human expressions of the respect that a society shows for the deceased and for the surviving family members." The Court further held that the State had a valid governmental interest in protecting the privacy of family members wishing to pay their final respects to the deceased.

2.5   Methods of Disposition

In the United States, there are a number of lawful methods of disposition of a dead body. Certainly, the most common is in-ground burial. Provided that the burial is on property dedicated as a public or private cemetery, it is lawful. In some rural areas, burial may be on private property, although the family may have to dedicate it as a family cemetery. Entombment may also be above ground where the body is placed in a mausoleum. In rare cases, such as Mao's tomb in China, the body may be indefinitely preserved for viewing.

As noted in Chapter Seven, cremation has gained wide acceptance in the United States as a method of disposition. Although cremation has been used for thousands of years by many cultures, it was infrequently utilized in the United States until the last fifty years. Provided the crematory is properly licensed and in compliance with state and local laws, the cremation of bodies is a perfectly legal form of disposition.

It must be noted that cremation is not technically a method of disposition, but actually one step in a mode of disposition. After the cremation and the processing of bone fragments, the cremated remains (which some refer to as cremains) will be collected and placed in an urn. Those cremated remains may be retained by the family, placed in a niche in a columbarium, entombed in a cemetery, or scattered. The scattering of cremated remains is usually confined to scattering gardens in cemeteries or at open sea. As cremation has become more popular, the government has restricted the scattering of cremains in public places and some inland waterways. Scattering of cremains in the ocean may be made at a distance of three nautical miles from the shoreline. Reports of the scattering must be filed with the Environmental Protection Agency.

Another emerging form of disposition which has been legalized in seven states as of 2011 is alkaline hydrolysis. This procedure entails placing a body in a cylinder that is filled with water and strong alkaline chemicals. Through a mixture of heat, agitation, and/or pressure, the body's tissues are hydrolyzed. Depending upon the level of heat, the process takes three to twelve hours, leaving calcified bone and a sterile liquid of amino acids, peptides, sugar and soap. The solution, which may have to be pretreated to lower the temperature and the pH level, can then be discharged into a sanitary sewer system. Like cremation, alkaline hydrolysis is not technically final disposition since it merely reduces the body to bones that are pulverized and placed in an urn or container for final disposition involving burial, scattering, or retention by the family.

Burial at sea is sometimes desired when a death takes place on land. Generally, no such burials are permitted on in-land waterways. Burial at sea may take place in the ocean at a distance of at least three nautical miles from the shoreline. In some designated areas, there are requirements on the depth of the water. Additionally, the body must be properly weighted in a special shroud to insure that the remains sink to the bottom rapidly and permanently.

Reports of all such burials must be made to the Environmental Protection Agency.

Another method of lawful disposition is the donation of the body to medical science. Because medical science requires dead bodies for dissection and study, each state in the country allows by statute for a decedent or a decedent's survivors to make a gift of decedent's body to medical science. The Uniform Anatomical Gift Act is discussed in greater detail in Chapter Four.

Chapter Three

RIGHTS OF PARTIES UNDERTAKING DISPOSITION

3.1   In General

The party who legally undertakes to dispose of a dead body is vested with certain rights and charged with certain duties: the rights and duties granted and imposed by law for the protection of the decedent's survivors and for the protection of the public. This paramount right to arrange the disposition of a dead body would indeed be empty and meaningless without a grant of certain specific rights necessary to effect disposition free from interference from others.

3.2   Right of Custody

A dead body is not property in the ordinary sense of the word, but it is a tangible object over which dominion is granted to the party undertaking the disposition. However, that right of custody is not absolute. Rather, it is a limited right, given for a specific purpose, and subject to revocation if the party possessing it does not exercise it or utilize it for a proper purpose. As stated by the Court in the case of *Pierce v. Proprietors of the Swan Point Cemetery*, 10 R.I. 227:

> "Although as we have said the body is not property in the usually recognized sense of the word, yet we may consider it as a sort of quasi-property to which certain persons may have rights, as they have duties to perform toward it, arising out of our common humanity. But the person having charge of it cannot be considered as the owner of it in any sense whatever; he holds it only as a sacred trust for the benefit of all who may from family or friendship have an interest in it, and we think that a court of equity may regulate it as such and change the custody if improperly managed."

The person exercising the right of disposition is granted the right to take possession and control of the body. The possession may be actual or constructive – actual possession where the body is physically within his custody and constructive possession where the body is physically in the custody of another. Thus, where the body is at the home of the next of kin, the possession is actual; where the body is at a hospital or mortuary, the custody of the next of kin is said to be constructive.

Custody of a dead body may be had only for the purpose of disposing of it in a lawful manner. As seen in Chapter Two, the failure to dispose of the body in a lawful manner not only takes away an individual's right of custody, but also can lead to criminal sanctions against such individual.

Possession and control of the body attaches from the moment of death and it may be continued for a reasonable length of time. The reasonableness of the length of time during which a body may be held pending final disposal is to be determined by the circumstances of the case. In the usual case several days may suffice. Under a different set of facts it may be necessary to withhold disposition for a longer time and such delay is not unwarranted where the cause is justifiable. In the case of death by contagious disease, however, the law may stipulate the maximum time during which the body may be held. In such cases the rule of reason is abrogated by the statutory provisions.

3.3　Right to Control the Funeral

The individual undertaking disposition has the power to exercise control over all matters relating to the funeral. He is free to choose whether to use a funeral home, which funeral home to use, what type of service, if any, will be held, what funeral merchandise will be purchased, and what the eventual method of disposition will be. In addition, the individual may arrange the time and place of burial convenient to the individual and disregard the feelings of others. In this respect, the individual is subject only to the regulations and rules of the crematory and cemetery.

The right to arrange the disposition is an exclusive right. In other words, if an individual has the paramount right of disposition, he or she is not compelled by law to share it with others. This being the case, the individual may elect to hold a private funeral and invite or exclude those whom he or she chooses.

For example, in the case of *Rader v. Davis*, 154 Iowa 306, 134 N.W. 849 (1912), a husband and wife had been divorced. The custody of the couple's only child was granted exclusively to the wife. When the child died, the wife refused to allow the husband to attend the funeral. The court upheld the wife's decision to exclude the husband, stating in part:

> "There was no duty, as we understand it, however, to conduct a public funeral, and if there were, private funerals are so common in this country that we would not feel disposed to say that public services are required to be held... There is no implied invitation to anyone to attend a funeral conducted from a private dwelling unless it be announced that such funeral is public, and even if so announced, the invitation may be revoked and anyone denied the right to attend whose presence might be objectionable."

The courts have made clear that the right to exclude others from the funeral extends even to services conducted in cemeteries. In *Ross v. Forest Law Memorial Park*, 199 Cal. Rptr. 854 (1984), the facts showed that the mother of the decedent instructed the cemetery that the funeral was to be restricted to invited guests only. The mother was especially concerned that unruly companions of her deceased 17 year old daughter would disturb the funeral. The cemetery orally agreed to take all reasonable steps to comply with the mother's request.

The funeral ceremony was completely disrupted by the decedent's friends. They attended the chapel services and the graveside services in outlandish outfits, which the Court described as "not in accord with traditional funeral attire." During the services, they drank and used cocaine, physically and verbally abused guests, and created a disturbance which had to be settled by the police. The mother sued the cemetery alleging negligence and breach of contract and claiming damages for mental and emotional distress.

The California Court of Appeals upheld the validity of the mother's complaint. The Court first noted that the mother, as next of kin to the daughter (the daughter had no spouse or children), had the right of disposition. The right of disposition, according to the Court, included "the right to determine the time, manner and place of burial." The Court then examined case law from other jurisdictions and concluded the right to determine the "manner" of burial gave the mother the right to exclude others from the funeral. In reaching this decision, the Appellate Court cited *Haney v. Stamper*, 277 Ky 1, 125 S.W. 2d 761 (1939), wherein it was held that a widow could rightfully exclude the decedent's brother from the funeral.

Since the mother had the right to exclude others from the funeral and since the cemetery had agreed to take steps to honor her wishes, the failure of the cemetery to take those steps constituted a breach of contract. Moreover, because the cemetery was aware that its failure to exclude the uninvited friends would cause mental and emotional injury to the mother, she could collect damages for her mental suffering.

The individual arranging the funeral may notify relatives and others at his will or he may elect not to do so. In *Seaton v. Commonwealth*, 149 Ky 498, 149 S.W. 871 (1912), the issue was addressed by the Court as follows:

> "Is appellate (the defendant) subject to punishment because he refused to permit his relatives and those of his wife or others to be notified so that they might be present at the interment? His relatives and friends may have regarded this conduct on his part as lack of consideration or respect for their feelings in the matter, but this is the extent of the bearing which his conduct in this particular can have upon the case. They have no legal right to be present. They may have been offended because not notified or invited, but no ground of complaint is afforded to the public on this account. In some localities funerals are not infrequently attended by invitations. Some are strictly private; while others are open to the public. Those are matters which address themselves to the discretion and will of those interested... the relatives and friends of the deceased."

If the next-of-kin wishes to exclude others from a visitation or a funeral, the funeral director is advised to impose certain conditions on the next-of-kin. First, if there is an obituary, it should note that the funeral services are private. No announcement of the time or place of the funeral ceremony should be made. The funeral director should also have the next-of-kin sign an indemnification form to cover any personal injury or property damage in the event the exclusion leads to violence. Finally, if a disruption by excluded family members is possible, the funeral director should require the next-of-kin to hire a security service to exclude uninvited individuals from the services.

3.4   Right to Choose Disposition

The paramount right to take custody of the body includes the right to choose the method of disposition. Therefore, the person found to have the paramount right has unfettered discretion in selecting if the decedent will be buried, cremated, or disposed of by some other method.

In *Dumouchelle v. Duke University*, 317 S.E. 2d 100 (N.C. App. 1984), the next of kin elected to have the decedent cremated. However, the executor of the decedent's will, noting that the will had expressed decedent's wish to buried in Ohio, countermanded the cremation order and had the decedent interred in Ohio. When the next of kin sued, the court held that, given the decedent's instruction in the will, the executor had the paramount right under North Carolina law to arrange the disposition. This being the case, his decision to bury the body rather than cremate it was well within his right.

3.5   Funeral Director with Right of Disposition

The lawful rights of the funeral director undertaking a funeral are primarily derived from two sources. There are those rights which are granted and imposed by statute and those arising from the funeral contract.

The former consists of those rights defined and provided by the statutes, ordinances and regulations of the jurisdiction where the funeral director practices. These are the laws and licensing regulations which authorize the funeral director to practice his profession. Generally, they empower him to take those actions which are incident to the funeral, *i.e.* transporting the dead, embalming, conducting funeral services, and arranging dispositions in cemeteries or crematories.

The second source of the funeral director's authority arises from the contract entered into between the funeral director and the individual with the paramount right of disposition. The funeral director has no rights in his professional capacity with respect to a dead body until such time as a valid contract is entered into between himself and another, either expressly or implicitly.

3.6   Funeral Contract

a.   In General

The funeral contract is an agreement between a funeral director and another competent party of legal age, whereby the consumer purchases and the funeral director agrees to furnish merchandise and services. The funeral contract may be oral or written. When the contract is oral, it may be expressed or implied. For example, when an individual dies in a nursing home and the family has left instructions to call a particular funeral home, that funeral home has an implied contract with that family to carry out the removal of the body.

The contract may be between the funeral home and the decedent's estate, his family, and/or an unrelated third party. Since, as will be discussed in Chapter Six, the decedent's estate is generally responsible for the decedent's funeral bill, it is an implied party to the contract. Funeral directors will often have the next of kin or surviving spouse execute the funeral contract also to show that the funeral home has authority to conduct the contracted services and to provide another source of payment in the event the estate is insolvent. Third parties that are unrelated to the decedent may also arrange for the funeral, such as employers, the armed forces, or government welfare agencies.

b.   Disclosures

In addition to the disclosures required by the FTC Funeral Rule (see Chapter Fourteen) and the Truth-in-Lending provisions (see Chapter Fifteen), some states have laws and regulations requiring that certain written disclosures must be given to the person making funeral arrangements. Generally, these disclosures are as follows: 1) the price of the funeral and a list of all services and merchandise included in the funeral; 2) the price of each supplemental item of service or merchandise; 3) a list of the cash advances made by the funeral director on behalf of the person making the funeral arrangements; and 4) the method of payment.

In states with these requirements, the funeral director may not simply enter into an oral funeral contract with the other party, but is required to give a written memorandum of the transaction. These disclosures are intended to be in the best interest of the consumer, but are also beneficial to the funeral director — the written contract is legally more sound, is explicit as to method of payment, is easier to prove in the case of default by the purchaser, and is proof of a valid contract.

c.   Contract Terminology

To insure that the contract is enforceable and in accordance with the state law prescribing certain disclosures and proscribing certain practices, the funeral director should use a contract form that has been reviewed and approved by legal counsel. This section describes provisions which are typically included in a standard funeral contract:

(1) **Itemization.** The FTC Funeral Rule requires price itemization of the components of the funeral services (i.e. the goods and services purchased). Some states also have statutes or rules requiring price itemization of funeral contracts. Therefore, the majority of the contract will spell out the goods and services purchased by the consumer.

(2) **Cash Transaction.** Most funeral homes stipulate in the contract that the sale is a cash transaction and not a credit transaction. Credit transactions involve many disclosures, which need not be made if the funeral home does not qualify as a creditor as defined in the Truth-in-Lending provisions.

(3) **Late Payment Charge or Penalty Charge.** A funeral home may charge a late payment charge or penalty charge for unanticipated late payment. If this charge is imposed, state law should be reviewed to determine if any ceiling to the penalty applies. An example of the penalty clause is as follows: "This is a CASH transaction due in full on (due date) and without exception becomes past due and delinquent on the due date. A penalty of _____ % per month (_____% per annum) on the unpaid balance for the unanticipated late payment will be charged effective (date)."

(4) **Collection Fees.** A contract may stipulate that in the event of default, the undersigned (person or persons making the funeral arrangements) agree to pay all costs of collection including reasonable attorney's fees. State law should be consulted to insure that a collection provision is permissible.

(5) **Estate Liability.** In many states the primary liability for payment of a funeral bill is the estate of the decedent (See Chapter Six). A funeral contract should include a statement that the person signing the contract is liable for payment of the funeral contract in addition to the liability imposed by law upon the estate. By doing this, the consumer signing the contract will be held responsible for payment in the event the estate is insolvent. Also, funeral homes may charge a late payment fee as stipulated in the contract even though the estate is liable for the payment of the contract. This charge could be substantial because many times payment is held up for several months on account of the administration of the estate.

(6) **Joint and Several (individual) Liability.** Directly above the signature line designated for the signature(s) of the person(s) making the funeral arrangements, the funeral home should include a statement similar to the one that follows: "I/we the undersigned, severally and jointly, hereby authorize the above funeral contract and promise to make payment thereof." With this statement the funeral home is holding all persons signing the contract jointly and individually liable for the payment of the funeral bill.

(7) **Disclaimer of Warranties.** A funeral contract may include a disclaimer of the implied warranties of merchantability and fitness for a particular purpose. These implied warranties basically mean that the casket and other goods sold will fulfill their intended uses, e.g. that the casket will be sufficient-

ly strong to hold the body and allow the body to be transported. If the bottom of the casket falls out, the warranty has been breached and the funeral director will be liable for damages.

To avoid liability for implied warranties, funeral directors may disclaim the warranties. The following statement may be used by the funeral director as a disclaimer of implied and expressed warranties:

"DISCLAIMER OF WARRANTIES

THE _____ FUNERAL HOME MAKES NO REPRESENTA-TIONS OR WARRANTIES REGARDING THE MERCHANDISE SOLD WITH THIS FUNERAL SERVICE. THE ONLY WARRANTIES, EXPRESSED OR IMPLIED, GRANTED IN CONNECTION WITH THE MERCHANDISE GOODS SOLD WITH THIS FUNERAL SERVICE ARE THE EXPRESS WRITTEN WARRANTIES, IF ANY, EXTENDED BY THE MANUFACTURERS THEREOF. NO OTHER WARRANTIES, EXPRESSED OR IMPLIED, INCLUDING THE IMPLIED WARRANTIES OF MERCHANTABILITY OR FITNESS FOR A PAR-TICULAR PURPOSE, ARE EXTENDED BY THE FUNERAL HOME."

Prior to disclaiming these warranties, funeral directors should consult state law to ensure that such a disclaimer is permissible. It is not lawful to disclaim these warranties in the District of Columbia and the twelve states of Alabama, Connecticut, Kansas, Maine, Maryland, Massachusetts, Minnesota, Mississippi, New Hampshire, Vermont, Washington, and West Virginia.

Many of the caskets and vaults sold by funeral directors have been warranted by the manufacturers of those caskets and vaults. While these warranties are extended to the consumers, funeral directors should ensure that consumers understand that the warranties are made by the manufacturer and not by the funeral home.

Chapter Four

WHO HAS THE RIGHT OF DISPOSITION

4.1   Introduction

As seen in the previous chapter, the paramount right of disposition provides an individual with broad authority in regard to the funeral and ultimate disposition of a dead body. What has not been addressed up to this point, however, is who is given this power. This is an issue of critical importance for the funeral director who will from time-to-time encounter family members in dispute as to the funeral and final disposition of a decedent. While generally the funeral director should not undertake to make legal decisions as to who has the paramount right of disposition, it is imperative that the funeral director have a firm understanding of this issue to avoid possible legal liability for improperly complying with the instructions of one who did not have the paramount right of disposition.

4.2   Right of Disposition Statutes

One of the more important developments in mortuary law over the past twenty years has been the widespread adoption by states of right of disposition laws that contain a priority list of who controls the funeral and disposition and provides mechanisms for resolving disputes. Forty-eight states now have laws on the books governing disposition rights. Although more than half of the laws do not contain all of the key components of an effective right of disposition law, over twenty of the laws, especially those that have been enacted in the past five years, provide comprehensive disposition elements and extensive protections for funeral homes.

An effective right of disposition statute has the following four primary components:

(1) A mechanism for an individual to control his or her disposition at the time of their death;

(2) A detailed priority list specifying who holds the right of disposition;

(3) A list of events and situations under which the right of disposition may be taken away; and

(4) Extensive protections and immunities for funeral homes and other death care providers.

4.3   Mechanism to Control Disposition

One of the primary components of state right of disposition laws is to give an individual the right to control the disposition of his or her own body upon death. In all states except Michigan (which does not give that right in its law) and Alaska and Hawaii (which do not have right of disposition statutes), an individual may leave binding disposition instructions or appoint an agent who has the power to make binding funeral and disposition arrangements. In about half of those states, an individual has the option of either leaving binding instructions or appointing an agent.

In thirty-seven states, the law allows an individual to leave binding funeral and disposition instructions. Most of those statutes specify that the instructions may be contained in a will, preneed contract, or other written instrument that is signed by the decedent and properly witnessed or notarized. A few states recognize that even oral instructions left by the decedent may be binding.

In thirty-four states, there is a mechanism in state law that allows an individual to appoint an agent or representative to make all funeral and disposition instructions. This appointed agent has superior rights even over the next-of-kin or spouse. The appointment instrument, which usually must be witnessed or notarized, will sometimes include the option for the decedent to specify funeral or disposition instructions that the agent is required to follow.

4.4   Priority List

Since most individuals do not take advantage of available legal mechanisms to plan disposition of their own remains, all right of disposition statutes contain a priority list specifying who holds the right to arrange the funeral and disposition. Typically, the priority list stipulates the surviving spouse, followed by adult children, parents, adult siblings, grandparents, and other relatives in a descending order of priority. In the absence of any relatives, state law may provide that a guardian or executor may execute the right. Effective right of disposition laws usually include a default provision at the end of the priority list which allows anyone, including the funeral director with custody of the body, to exercise the right of disposition if there are no family members willing or available.

4.5 Forfeiture of Right of Disposition

While a priority list helps to provide necessary guidance so that families and funeral homes can decide who has the authority to make funeral and disposition arrangements, an effective right of disposition statute also needs to include several key components to address conflicts and uncertainties. These key components include the following:

a. Missing Relatives

One of the most important features of an effective right of disposition law is a provision that takes away the right of disposition from any person who cannot be located. If an individual cannot be located after using reasonable efforts, that missing person loses the right of disposition and the funeral home may make arrangements with other individuals who are lower on the priority list. This is a helpful provision because it allows the funeral and disposition to take place within a reasonable amount of time without the need to hold off arrangements until missing relatives are located. Approximately 40% of the states have a provision which disqualifies the right of a person who cannot be located.

b. Majority Control

In several of the classes on the priority list, there are often two or more individuals who hold equal rights. For example, if a widow dies, there may be several children who hold equal rights to control the disposition. State laws with majority control provisions allow a majority of those who hold the right to control the disposition. This brings certainty to the funeral and disposition arrangements and allows the funeral and disposition to proceed, even though an individual in the minority may object to the funeral and disposition arrangements. Approximately half of the states have provisions that allow a majority in a particular class to control the disposition over the contrary wishes of a minority.

c. Waiver of Uncooperative Relatives

It is not unusual for funeral homes to face relatives who hold the right of disposition but who will not cooperate in making arrangements. In about thirty percent of the states, the law takes away the right of disposition from an individual who does not actively exercise the right within a specified time period. Typically, the time period specified may be anywhere from 48 to 72 hours. Once that time period has expired, the funeral home may proceed to persons down the priority list to persons who are willing to make funeral arrangements.

d. Homicide Cases

If an individual who holds the right of disposition is arrested for criminally causing the death of the decedents whose disposition he or she controls, it is nearly impossible to make arrangements with that individual. Effective right of disposition laws take away the right of someone who is arrested for criminally causing the death of the person over whom he or she holds the right of disposition. Currently, approximately one third of the states have a disqualification provision tied to homicide.

4.6 Protection for Funeral Homes

There are three primary protections that funeral homes want to include in a right of disposition statute. The three are the right to rely, the ability to recover costs, and comprehensive immunity provisions.

The right to rely involves provisions in the law which grants the funeral home the ability to rely upon the representations of a family member. The provisions typically relieve the funeral home from any duty to independently investigate the truthfulness of a family member's claim or to search for missing relatives. For example, in a recent case of *Mack v. Brown*, 919

N.Y.S.2nd 166 (2011) an individual was cremated by a New York funeral home who relied upon a cremation authorization signed by a person claiming to be the decedent's wife. Subsequent to the cremation, the decedent's first wife sued the funeral home claiming that she and the decedent were never divorced, and therefore, the person claiming to be the second wife was not legally married to the decedent. Noting comprehensive immunity provisions in the New York law, the court held that the funeral home was immune from civil liability since they relied in good faith upon the directions of the person who claimed to be the lawfully wedded second wife. The court further held that the funeral home was under no legal obligation to investigate the marital status of the person claiming to be the second wife.

When disputes emerge against competing family members and the funeral home is caught in the middle, it is very helpful to the funeral home if the right of disposition statute specifically authorizes the funeral home to stop all funeral and disposition arrangements until the dispute is settled. States with comprehensive protections for funeral homes go a step further and authorize the funeral home to recover embalming and refrigeration costs which may be incurred as a result of the delay caused by the dispute. Some states even allow the funeral home to recover their legal costs if they have to initiate court proceedings to resolve the dispute.

The last of the triad of protections is a broad immunity provision which protects a funeral home from criminal, civil, or disciplinary claims if they have relied in good faith upon representations of family members that may later prove to be untrue. Some states require that a funeral home receive the representations in writing in order to take advantage of immunity provisions. Therefore, it is always advisable to document in cremation authorization forms and other representations that the person providing disposition direction claims to have the right of disposition and is not aware of anyone with a superior or equal right.

4.7   Anatomical Gift Act

In response to the need to promote organ donation and other anatomical gifts, the Uniform Anatomical Gift Act has been enacted in all fifty states and the District of Columbia. Since this statute is based upon a model law, most states have the identical statute. Some states have enacted minor changes into the Uniform Act.

The Act generally provides that any individual of sound mind and legal age may donate all or part of his body upon his death. The person may designate the gift in his Last Will and Testament. The gift is effective upon death without waiting for probate. If the will is invalid for any reason, the gift is valid to the extent it was acted upon in good faith.

A donation may also be made by a document other than a will. The document must be signed by the individual in the presence of two witnesses. Many states have a prescribed form for the gift. Also, many states have statutorily provided that a person may legally use the reverse side of a valid drivers license as a donation form.

In addition to the decedent, the Uniform Anatomical Gift Act also authorizes the surviving spouse and the next of kin to make donations of the decedent's body. As with the paramount right of disposition, there is a priority in who has the power to make a gift. The first priority is the surviving spouse, followed by the adult son or daughter, either parent, an adult brother or sister, a guardian of the decedent at the time of his death, or any other person authorized or under obligation to dispose of the body.

The relative may make a gift of all or part of the decedent's body if there are no contrary indications by the decedent or if there is no opposition by a member of the same class or a relative with a higher priority. In the event notice of these contrary indications or opposition has been given or is known by the donee, the donee may not accept the gift.

The gift may be made to any donee authorized by the Act to accept donations. These donees typically include hospitals, accredited medical or dental schools, surgeons, physicians, medical storage banks, and designated persons needing therapy or transplantations. The donee must employ the gift for medical or dental research, education or the advancement of medical science or therapy.

Where the gift is of the entire body, the surviving spouse or next-of-kin may, subject to the terms of the gift, authorize embalming and the use of the body in a funeral service. Likewise, where the gift is a part of the body, the remainder may, after removal of the donated part, be delivered to the surviving spouse, next of kin or other person for disposition. The Act provides that any person acting in good faith compliance with the Act shall not be liable for damages in a civil action or subject to prosecution in a criminal action.

Unlike the issue regarding the paramount right of disposition, there is no question regarding the supremacy of a gift made under the Uniform Anatomical Gift Act. That donation takes precedence over any contrary wishes of the survivors. Provided that the gift has been made in compliance with the legal requirements of the Act, no relative can supersede the gift.

Chapter Five

DUTIES OF THE FUNERAL DIRECTOR

5.1   In General

The funeral director in carrying out the preparation of the body and the direction of the funeral service is under various legal and contractual duties. The sources of these duties are the statutory laws of the state, the requirements of the funeral contract, and the common law. If the funeral director violates these duties, he will incur liability to the state and/or the family of the decedent.

5.2   Statutory Duties

a.   Permits

In nearly all jurisdictions, the funeral director is required to obtain permits from appropriate authorities to arrange for the proper disposition of the dead. Typically, this involves obtaining a death certificate, burial permit and transit permit. State and municipal statutes and regulations which require these permits have been upheld by courts as reasonable exercises by the state of its police power to protect the health of the public. In *Meyers v. Clarke*, 122 Ky. 866, 90 S.W. 1049 (1906), the court found that a regulation of the municipal Department of Health requiring a burial permit to be issued before a decedent could be interred was a reasonable measure to prevent the spread of contagious diseases in the city and to protect the general health of the inhabitants.

Several states have implemented electronic death certificate registration systems with varying degree of success. The mechanics and contents of death certificates, burial permits, cremation permits and transit permits are not within the province of this volume.

b.   Health Laws and Regulations.

There are a number of statutes and health regulations which regulate the practice of embalming and funeral directing, some of which are discussed in later chapters of this volume. However, with regard to the proper handling, preparation and burial of bodies, the funeral director will have to be aware of the relevant statutes and regulations in his jurisdiction. States and municipalities differ widely in the regulation of embalming and burial.

For example, half of the states have laws or regulations which require embalming under certain circumstances. In states like Arizona, Colorado, Delaware, Idaho, Oklahoma, South Dakota, and Texas, a body must be embalmed, refrigerated, buried or cremated within 24 hours of death. Other states impose a less stringent time limit such as Iowa at 48 hours,

Massachusetts at 50 hours, and Minnesota at 72 hours. Still other states, like Kansas and Maine, require embalming if the body is to be transported by common carrier. The funeral director must, of course, be completely cognizant of these laws not only to maintain compliance with state and local law, but to properly represent to funeral consumers what the law does and does not require with regard to embalming, refrigeration and disposition.

5.3   Contractual Obligations

When the funeral director enters into the funeral contract, whether oral or written, he promises to undertake certain obligations. If the funeral director breaches these obligations, he is liable for the damages that follow as a result of his breach. These damages, more often than not, involve the emotional distress that can result to survivors when the services of the funeral director are not carried out as promised. The recovery of these damages is discussed more fully in Section 5.5 on mental anguish.

The funeral contract imposes numerous duties on the funeral director, some implied and others expressed. Although it is not possible to detail all of the possible contractual breaches that can arise, the student of mortuary law should be familiar with the following breaches which often may end up in litigation.

a.   *Negligent Embalming.*

When a funeral director contracts to embalm a body, he undertakes to use the skill and care of a reasonably prudent and careful person skilled in the art of embalming. If the embalming falls short of that standard of care, the funeral director will be liable for the damages that result therefrom.

For example, in *Thompson v. the Duncan Bros. Funeral Homes, Inc.*, 116 Misc.2d 227, 445 N.Y.S.2d 324 (1982), the casket was opened for the family and the remains were found to be decomposed, swollen, odoriferous and leaking fluid. The court awarded members of the family $35,000.00 to compensate them for the personal injuries they suffered upon witnessing the results of the negligent embalming.

In a California case, a funeral home was held liable for the alleged negligent embalming of the plaintiff's father. In this case, the decedent's body was shipped from California to Oklahoma. Upon arrival in Oklahoma, the body was "in a decayed condition, malodorous and dripping fluid." The court held that "the mental and emotional shock suffered by the plaintiffs upon learning that the body was in such a condition made them ill, (and was) an element of compensable injury." *Carey v. Lima, Salmon and Tully Mortuary*, 168 Cal.App.2d 42, 335 P.2d 181, 182 (1959).

b.   *Negligent Funeral Directing.*

The failure of a funeral director to perform the many duties involved in directing the funeral service will give to liability. In *Golston v. Lincoln Cemetery, Inc.*, 573 S.W.2d 700 (1978 Mo.App.), a funeral director who had failed to properly supervise the burial at the cemetery, thereby permitting the decedent to be buried in a shallow grave and without the vault that the contract provided for, was held liable for breach of contract. The court not only awarded damages for mental anguish suffered by the family, but also imposed punitive damages against the funeral director.

Similarly, in *Wilson v. Ferguson*, 747 S.W. 2d 499 (Tex. Ap. 1988), the facts showed that when the funeral procession arrived for the graveside ceremony, the grave had not been properly prepared. Rather than assisting the family, the funeral home employees "left the gravesite saying they were in a hurry for another funeral." When the body was later damaged at the cemetery, the court held that the funeral home had breached its contractual duty to perform its services with ordinary care.

In *Lamm v. Shingleton*, 231 N.C. 1, 55 S.E.2d 810 (1949), a funeral director was held liable for the mental distress suffered by a surviving spouse upon learning that mud and water had entered into a vault containing her husband's casket. The vault had leaked because the funeral director had failed to lock the vault properly.

In *Clark v. Smith*, 494 S.W.2d 192 (Tex. 1973), the employee of the defendant was instructed by the plaintiffs to hold the dead body until they decided what funeral director to call. When the defendant had possession of the body, it underwent drastic putrefactive changes. Although the defendant was never instructed to embalm the body, there was explicit testimony that he should take the body and keep it in a suitable condition pending burial. The plaintiffs brought suit for mental anguish suffered at the appearance of the decedent as a result of defendant's negligence in not keeping the body suitable for burial, in not using preservative fluids, in not refrigerating the body in order to preserve it, and in not informing the plaintiffs as to what was necessary to preserve the body to keep it suitable for a decent burial, all of which were proximate causes of the plaintiffs' mental anguish. The court held that the above allegations constituted negligent breaches of a duty owed by the funeral director to the decedent's family.

Funeral directors may also be liable for failure to honor requests made by the family. For example, in *Meyer v. Nottger*, 241 N.W.2d 911 (Iowa 1976), the complaint alleged, among other things, that the funeral director had improperly refused to allow the plaintiffs to view the body and had failed to comply with his agreement to delay the funeral procession until the plaintiffs could arrive at the funeral. As a result, the plaintiffs were unable to attend the burial which they alleged resulted in mental anguish and, in one case, a heart attack. The court found that these allegations were legally sufficient to allow a jury to decide the case.

Substantial liability can be imposed for what appear to be minor errors of judgment. In a Washington case, the surviving spouse had requested that her husband be buried wearing his favorite cowboy hat. When the funeral director returned the hat to a different relative rather than complying with the request, the jury awarded the spouse $100,000.

c. Safeguard the Body.

Although cases of mentally deranged people sexually assaulting or harming bodies are rare occurrences, a funeral home may be liable for such generally unforeseen occurrences if it does not take reasonable precaution to safeguard the body. In *Draper Mortuary v. Superior Court*, 135 Cal.App.3d 533, 185 Cal.Rptr. 396 (1982), a person entered through an unlocked chapel door and sexually assaulted the body which was lying in state. Although the defendant claimed there was no history of such prior occurrences which would have forewarned him to take safeguards against such intrusions, the court rejected that defense and found the funeral home liable for violating its special duty of care that exists between a mortuary and a bereaved family who leaves the remains of their loved one in the care and custody of the funeral home.

d. Privacy.

If funeral directors fail to comply with the survivor's requests for confidentiality regarding the death or for privacy during the funeral arrangements, they can be held liable for breach of contract. In *Fitzsimmons v. Olinger Mortuary Ass'n*, 91 Colo. 544, 17 P.2d 535 (1982), a funeral director was requested to transport a body and prepare it for burial without any undue publicity. When the funeral director photographed the body and used it in advertisement, the court held that the funeral director had violated an expressed and implied promise not to violate the confidentiality of the family. The fact that the court found a violation of an implied promise suggests that the funeral director would have been liable for violating the confidentiality of the family even had the family not requested that the funeral director avoid any undue publicity.

The courts have also upheld a family's right to request a cemetery, and presumably a funeral director, to exclude unwanted visitors from the funeral and burial. In *Ross v. Forest Lawn Memorial Park,* 199 Cal. Rptr. 854 (1984), the family had requested the cemetery to take appropriate measures to keep the graveside service private and to exclude a certain group of unwanted friends of the decedent. When the cemetery failed to take the appropriate measures and the graveside service was interrupted by the unwanted friends, the cemetery was held liable for breach of contract and the damages which resulted therefrom.

e. Defective Merchandise.

Funeral directors, as purveyors of merchandise, are held to the same implied warranties that other merchants are. By law these implied warranties, which include the implied warranties of "merchantability" and "fitness for a particular purpose," involve promises that the products are fit for the ordinary and particular purpose for which such goods are used. Unless these warranties are properly disclaimed (see Sections 3.6 and 15.3), the funeral director will be liable if the merchandise, e.g. caskets and vaults, prove defective.

For example, in *Estate of Harper v. Orlando Funeral Home, Inc.*, 366 So.2d 126 Fla. App. 1979), a funeral director was held to have breached an implied warranty of merchantability and fitness for a particular purpose when a casket holding the body fell apart as it was being transported to the grave. Likewise, in *McDaniel v. Bass-Smith Funeral Home, Inc.*, 80 N.C. App. 629, 343 S.E.2d 228 (1986), a funeral home was found liable for supplying a casket that would not close properly. The evidence of the unworkmanlike condition was supported by findings that the defendant's employees experienced difficulty closing the casket before funeral services and that one corner of the casket was not closed during the services, thereby allowing the deceased's remains to be visible. The court allowed the plaintiff to recover for emotional anguish under these facts.

In *Cottom v. McGuire Funeral Service, Inc.*, 262 A.2d 807 (D.C. 1970), a handle fell off a casket while it was being carried by a pallbearer. He was injured as a result and sued the funeral director, alleging that the casket was defective. The lower court dismissed the complaint because it found that the pallbearer was not the intended "user" of the product and, therefore, the funeral director owed him no duty of care to provide a safe product. The Appellate Court reversed, however, and held that the pallbearer was indeed the intended "user" of the casket. The funeral director was held liable for supplying a defective product which violated the implied warranties of merchantability and fitness for a particular purpose.

f. Transportation

A funeral home supplying the hearse and limousine for the conveyance of the body and the mourners respectively is a private carrier and, as such, is charged with the legal duty to transport its passengers in a safe and non-negligent manner. If the funeral home fails to exercise ordinary care in carrying out the transportation and, as a result thereof, a passenger is injured, the funeral home will be liable for breach of contract.

In order for the funeral home to be liable, it is necessary to show the negligent driver of the vehicle was an agent of the funeral home. In other words, if the driver is an employee of the funeral home or if the funeral home engages a limousine service and represents such cars to be owned by the funeral home, it will be liable for the negligence of such drivers. In *Sack v. A. R. Nunn & Son*, 129 O.S. 128 (1934), the Supreme Court of Ohio held that a funeral director who had undertaken by contract to transport a family could not relieve himself from the negligence of the driver by showing that he engaged another to perform the transportation, especially when the family had no notice that the transportation service was being rendered by someone other than the funeral director or one under his control.

On the other hand, if there is no agency relationship between the driver and the funeral director, liability will not be imposed. In *Pantall v. Schriver*, 135 O.S. 164 (1939), a volunteer driving his own vehicle in a funeral procession caused injury to his passengers due to negligence. The court relieved the funeral director of any liability because there was no showing that the negligent driver was under the control or direction of the funeral director.

g. Aftercare.

Aftercare refers to grief counseling, support groups, or other grief facilitation activities sponsored by funeral homes. In the past twenty years, many funeral directors have begun programs in this very worthwhile and valuable service.

While no cases have been brought against funeral homes arising out of aftercare activities, there is a risk of some type of malpractice action. Similar claims have been brought against priests and ministers who attempted to counsel individuals and failed to recognize suicidal tendencies. For example, in *Nally v. Grace Community Church*, 157 Cal. App. 3d 912 (1984) the court allowed a family to bring a malpractice action against their minister alleging that he failed to prevent the suicide of one he was counseling. To avoid such claims, funeral homes sponsoring aftercare activities should undertake the following precautions:

(1) Do not refer to grief counseling as therapy or the counselor as a therapist. Terminology such as grief facilitator is recommended.

(2) All funeral home employees that participate in the aftercare program should have grief facilitation training.

(3) The grief facilitator should be trained to refer any serious or apparently serious problems to a psychologist or psychiatrist.

(4) The grief counseling or aftercare program should be covered by the funeral home's malpractice insurance.

5.4 Tort Liability

Funeral directors have to comply with duties and obligations that arise by operation of law as well as those that arise out of the funeral contract. When there is a violation of these duties with resulting damages, a tort has been committed and the court will award damages to those who suffer as a result of the violation of the legal duty.

Two duties recognized by the law which impact directly on the funeral director are: (1) the duty not to interfere with the right of burial; and (2) the duty of exercising reasonable care to keep the funeral home premises or other places under the control of the funeral director in a reasonably safe condition. Violations of these duties that result in damages will make the funeral director liable in tort. The remainder of this section will review those torts that are likely to result from violations of these duties:

a. Wrongfully Withholding a Body.

The common law generally recognizes that the surviving spouse or the next of kin has the right to the custody of the body, in the condition that it was left in by death, and that such person has the right to bury it without inter-ference. The refusal to release the body by a funeral director who has pre-pared it for burial until he has been paid for his services is widely recognized as an actionable violation of the family's right to burial without interference. For example, in *Morgan v. Richmond*, 336 So.2d 342 (1976), a funeral direc-tor who withheld the body of plaintiff's deceased mother until payment was made was liable for damages resulting from the humiliation, embarrassment and mental distress suffered by the plaintiff. A similar result was reached in *Levite Undertakers Co. v. Griggs*, 495 So. 2d 63 (Ala. 1986), where the court found the refusal to release the body "morally reprehensible".

b. *Loss of the Body.*

There have been cases where the funeral home has misidentified bod-ies and the funeral home incorrectly interred the wrong one. For example, in *Holsen v. Heritage Mut. Ins. Co.*, 165 Wis. 2d 641, 478 N.W. 2d 59 (1991), the funeral home had mixed-up two bodies and had the plaintiff's father wrongful-ly interred. When the body was not available for the visitation, the court found that the funeral home had negligently interfered with the family's common law right to properly conduct a funeral.

c. Mutilation of the Body.

The right of possession of the body for the purpose of burial carries with it the right to receive the body in the condition it was in at the time of death. If the body is mutilated, a tort is committed.

Mutilation, although slight and necessary, is involved in embalming a body. Generally, a funeral director has the right to do this as the mutilation is implicitly sanctioned by the permission given to embalm the body. If, howev-er, the embalming is done without permission, the tort of mutilation of the body occurs.

In *Sworski v. Simons*, 208 Minn. 201, 293 S.W. 309 (1940), a funeral director received an unidentified body from a coroner who advised him to embalm the body. The funeral director followed that advice and embalmed the body before the next of kin could be located. When the next of kin learned of the embalming, he sued the funeral director for mutilation of the body. Because the embalming had not been authorized by the next of kin, the court permitted the plaintiff to bring the action. The court held that it was not a defense for the funeral director to claim that the embalming was beneficial.

In *Scheuer v. William F. Howard Funeral Home*, 385 S. 2d 1076 (Fla. 1980), the funeral home embalmed without permission and in violation of the decedent's Jewish faith. The funeral director testified that he "was aware the deceased was of the Jewish faith and because of such knowledge saved two bottles of blood to be buried with her." The court permitted the plaintiff to bring an action finding that there was an issue for the jury to decide as to whether the funeral director was aware of the adverse consequences of his decision to immediately embalm the body.

A second, although less likely, incidence of mutilation involving funeral directors can occur with unauthorized autopsies. An autopsy is a post-mortem examination of the body, usually for the purposes of determining the cause of death. If the autopsy is not authorized by the next of kin or is not duly ordered by the coroner in the lawful discharge of his duties, it constitutes an actionable tort.

Although funeral directors do not typically conduct the autopsy, they still may be liable if they participate in it or consent to it without the authorization of the next of kin. The court in *Myers v. Clarke*, 122 Ky. 866, 90 S.W. 1049 (1906) held that funeral directors who, without permission of the next of kin, permitted autopsies to be performed will be jointly liable with the person performing the autopsy. Likewise in *Palenske v. Bruning*, 98 Ill. App. 644 (1900), a funeral director who assisted in an unauthorized autopsy was held jointly liable.

However, if the funeral director merely accedes to the demands of the coroner and makes the body available, he will not be liable if the subsequent autopsy is not authorized. This was recognized by decision in *Konecny v. Hohenschuh*, 188 Iowa 1075, 173 N.W. 901 (1919) and *Gurganious v. Simpson*, 213 N.C. 613, 197 S.E. 163 (1938). The courts are in an apparent agreement that funeral directors are not required to challenge the coroner's authority to conduct the autopsy in order to avoid possible liability for participating or consenting to an unauthorized autopsy.

d. *Injury to Invitees.*

A funeral home owes the duty of care to each invitee to the funeral home to maintain the premises in a reasonably safe condition for its intended use. The chapel, staterooms, means of ingress and egress, restrooms and other facilities must be maintained in a reasonably safe condition in order that such invitees in the exercise of ordinary care will not suffer injury.

The degree of the duty of care a landowner owes to a person on the landowner's property depends on the status of the person. A high degree of care is owed to one who has been invited on the property by the land owner; on the other hand, a trespasser is owed a very little degree of care. Persons coming to a funeral home for the purpose of attending funerals, viewing remains, or engaging the funeral director's services have generally been recognized to be "invitees" and, therefore, entitled to a high degree of care. Moreover, some courts have heightened that duty of care with funeral homes, reasoning that because invitees to a funeral home are often in an emotionally disturbed state, funeral directors should expect that they will be somewhat less prudent in looking out for themselves than the ordinary man would be.

An example of the above rule was found in *Shipman v. Norton*, 154 Cal. App. 2d 90, 315 P.2d 906 (1957), where the plaintiff injured herself when stepping off a porch onto a step which was made in the same brick pattern material as the porch. The plaintiff claimed the funeral home was negligent in not differentiating the step from the porch. The funeral home defended against the claim by alleging that the plaintiff was contributory negligent since she had seen the step on her way into the funeral home and should have remembered it on her way out. The court held for the plaintiff, finding that if an undifferentiated step was negligent in other contexts, it should be considered even more so in a funeral home situation where it is to be expected that invitees will be emotionally upset after services and not looking out for themselves.

Funeral directors are required by this duty of care to take precaution against snow and ice, especially during services when people will be coming in and out of the funeral home. In both *Watts v. Rhodes*, 325 Mass. 697, 91 N.E.2d 925 (1950) and *Filipiak v. Plombon*, 15 Wis.2d 483, 113 N.W.2d 365 (1962), funeral homes were found liable for injuries resulting from icy walkways and ramps leading to and from the funeral home.

e.   *Injury to Pallbearers and Clergy.*

A funeral director will be liable for an injury suffered by a pallbearer (those who voluntarily carried the casket) or a member of the clergy if the injury is caused by the tort of the funeral director. In *Frederick v. J.E. Hixson and Sons*, 159 So.2d 599 (La. 1964), a minister presiding at graveside service was injured when he slipped on artificial grass mats covering a marble slab. Although the grass mats had been negligently placed on the marble slabs by the vault company, the funeral director was found jointly liable. The court held that the funeral director had full responsibility to control the funeral, which responsibility included the "prior discovery of reasonably discoverable conditions of the premises that may be unreasonably dangerous and correction thereof or a warning to the invitee of the danger". By failing to take proper steps to see that the gravesite was reasonably safe or at least warn those attending the burial services of the hazard, the funeral director breached the duty of care he owed the invitees.

In *Kennedy v. Ricker Funeral Home, Inc.,* 119 N.H. 827, 409 A.2d 778 (1979), the defendant funeral director was held liable for injuries incurred by the plaintiff pallbearer when the pallbearer fell while carrying a handleless casket into the church. An employee of the funeral home asked the plaintiff to help carry the casket into the church and negligently failed to instruct the plaintiff as to how to carry the handleless casket, which by design required the pallbearers to place their fingers in a groove that ran along the sides. While carrying the casket the pallbearer slipped, lost his grip on the casket, and consequently suffered injury to his knee. During the trial there was expert testimony that handleless caskets tend to be unstable and that the defendant had in the past given instructions to people carrying caskets both with and without handles. Thus, the court found that defendant had the duty to instruct the pallbearer in the use of handleless caskets and that he was negligent for failing to do so.

5.5   Mental Anguish

   a.   Physical Impact.

As a general rule, courts are very reluctant to award damages that cannot be measured with some precision. For this reason, it was traditionally recognized that plaintiffs could not recover monetary damages merely for mental distress or anguish suffered as a result of a contract breach or tort. The courts required some other physical indicia of injury before permitting a plaintiff the right to seek recovery for mental anguish.

The necessity of showing physical injury prior to any recovery for mental anguish is slowly being eroded in American law. This erosion has taken place in many areas. For example, in jurisdictions that still recognize this rule, the requirements have generally been changed from physical injury to physical impact. Thus, it is only necessary to show that there has been some physical impact rather than injury as a threshold to recover damages for mental anguish.

Erosion of the physical impact rule has also occurred in certain areas of the law. Nowhere is this more evident than in actions against funeral directors for contract breaches or torts. Courts have taken great pains to create exceptions to the physical impact rule or even to abandon it in order to permit plaintiffs to bring actions against funeral directors. Citing the fact that plaintiffs who have been wronged by funeral directors often have little or no other damages to seek other than damage from mental anguish, courts have devised numerous ways around the physical impact rule.

   b.   Intentional Infliction of Mental Distress.

As the physical impact rule has been eroded, courts have begun to recognize the tort of intentional infliction of mental distress. This tort permits recovery of damages for mental anguish by the plaintiff when the defendant's conduct is "intentional, wrongful, outrageous, reckless and malicious and done with the intention of causing plaintiff severe emotional distress." *Meyer v. Nottger*, 241 N.W.2d 911 (Iowa 1976).

In explaining this exception, the court in *Estate of Harper v. Orlando Funeral Home, Inc.*, 36 So.2d 126 (Fla. App. 1979), held that absent a physical impact, mental anguish for negligent funeral directing could not be recovered unless plaintiffs allege that defendant's conduct exceeded all bounds reasonably tolerated by society such as to suggest malice or the entire want of care or great indifference. Another Florida court held that such an allegation had been made in *Scherer v. Rubin Memorial Chapel Ltd.*, 444 So.2d 1176 (Fla. App. 1984), wherein the complaint alleged that the defendant funeral director had put a body other than the decedent's in the decedent's casket and burial clothes, that when confronted with this error, the defendant tried to convince the plaintiff that the body in question was indeed the decedent, and that after removing the burial clothes from the wrong body, the defendant simply threw the clothes over the decedent's unprepared body. The court ruled that the allegation in the complaint implied sufficient malice to permit recovery for pain, suffering and mental anguish.

c. Contractual Breaches.

Courts in some jurisdictions have relied on the unique nature of funeral contracts to carve out an exception to the physical impact rule. In *Lamm v. Shingleton*, 231 N.C. 10, 55 S.E.2d 810 (1949), the court, noting the personal nature of the funeral contract and the fact that the contract itself puts the funeral director on notice that a breach thereof would probably result in mental anguish, held the damages from mental anguish could be awarded in cases involving breaches of funeral contracts.

The same rationale was applied in *Meyer v. Nottger,* 241 N.W.2d 911 (Iowa 1976), wherein the court permitted recovery for mental anguish as a result of a contractual breach even in the absence of physical trauma because the contract in question was not concerned with trade and commerce, but with life and death and matters of mental concern and solicitude, which should have put the funeral director on notice that mental anguish would result from his breach.

An additional justification for the exception to the physical impact rule was provided for in *Allen v. Jones*, 104 Cal. Ap. 3d 207, 163 Cal Rptr. 445 (1980). After reciting the fact that the funeral director should be on notice that mental anguish will result from his breach, the court added that the award of damages for mental distress against the funeral director serves as a useful and necessary means to maintain professional standards in the funeral industry. It added that damage for mental anguish is often the only method to compensate victims of wrongful acts by funeral directors.

d. Negligent Infliction of Mental Distress.

As seen earlier, courts now generally recognize that damages for mental anguish can be recovered when the defendant's wrongful conduct is so malicious or reckless that it appears intentionally calculated to cause mental anguish in plaintiffs. Some courts have gone beyond that theory and now permit the recovery of damages for mental anguish in those cases where the wrongful conduct consists merely of simple negligence. In justifying this exception, the courts often use the same rationale as with the funeral contract exception, i.e. funeral directors are on notice that negligent conduct will produce mental anguish and damages for mental anguish are often the only method to compensate victims for such wrongful conduct.

In *Corrigal v. Ball & Dodd Funeral Home, Inc.*, 89 Wash. 2d 959, 577 P.2d 580 (1978), the Washington Supreme Court permitted an action for negligent infliction of mental distress against a funeral director. The court held that proof of simple negligence, as opposed to malicious or reckless conduct, was sufficient to recover damages for mental anguish. A similar result was reached in *Holsen v. Heritage Mut. Ins. Co.*, 165 Wis. 2d 641, 478 N.W. 2d 59 (1991), where the court held that a funeral director could be sued in Wisconsin under the theory of negligent infliction of emotional distress.

Fortunately, those states permitting funeral directors to be sued for negligent infliction of emotional distress are still in the minority. The majority of jurisdictions refuse to permit this action to be brought against funeral directors absent some evidence of intentional misconduct or physical impact. Such was the result in *Audia v. Rossi Bros. Funeral Home, Inc.*, 140 Ohio App. 3d 589 (7th Cir. 2000). That case involved a funeral home's mistake in switching bodies in setting up two visitations. Although the Ohio Court of Appeals recognized that the Ohio Supreme Court had permitted cases to be brought for intentional infliction of emotional distress, it refused to allow an action for the negligent infliction of emotional distress. Moreover, it held that Ohio law did not recognize an exception even when the allegations involved the negligence handling of a dead body.

> e. *Punitive Damages.*

Punitive damages are awarded by a court to a plaintiff not to compensate the plaintiff for damages suffered, but to punish the defendant. For this reason, punitive damages are not awarded in cases of simple negligence where the defendant unintentionally caused an injury. They are given only in those cases when the defendant's conduct has been so outrageous as to justify punishment.

These principles have been applied in cases dealing with wrongful conduct of funeral directors. In *Allen v. Jones*, 104 Cal. App.3d 207, 163 Cal. Rptr. 445 (1980), the complaint alleged that the defendant negligently shipped the cremated remains of the plaintiff's brother, thereby causing the cremains to be lost. The court dismissed the claim in the complaint for punitive damages, holding that punitive damages could not be recovered in a case involving simple negligence.

In *Meyer v. Nottger*, 241 N.W.2d 911 (Iowa 1976), however, the court permitted the plaintiff to seek punitive damages because they had alleged wrongful conduct that was committed with a willful and reckless disregard to the rights of others. Also, in *Golston v. Lincoln Cemetery, Inc.*, 573 S.W.2d 700 (Mo. App. 1978), an award of punitive damages was upheld by an Appellate Court because it found that the defendant had shown a complete indifference to or a conscious disregard of the emotional well-being of the plaintiff.

It should be noted that because punitive damages are awarded only in cases of willful or very reckless conduct, it is normally against public policy to insure against this conduct. In other words, most liability insurance policies will not cover awards of punitive damages. Therefore, while funeral director's liability insurance will normally cover damages arising out of the funeral director's negligence, any recovery of punitive damages must be personally paid by the funeral home.

Chapter Six

LIABILITY FOR FUNERAL EXPENSES

6.1   In General

While the care of the family and the proper performance of his duties are the principal concerns of the funeral director, as a responsible entrepreneur, he or she also has an obligation to the funeral home. In order to maintain the economic survival of that enterprise, a funeral director must be able to collect funeral bills in a timely manner. It is therefore his or her responsibility to ascertain who will pay for the funeral and to ensure that person is legally bound to make that payment.

The funeral home has a number of potential sources to look to for the payment of the funeral bill: the estate of the decedent, the surviving spouse, a parent (if the decedent is a minor), any person who signs the contract with the funeral home, or, in the last resort, the government. As seen in this chapter, the legal liability of these various parties will depend on a number of factors. The prudent funeral director will ensure that a solvent party has a legal obligation to pay for the funeral before he agrees to render such services.

6.2   Liability of the Estate

a.   Primary Obligor.

When a person dies, the real and personal property owned by him at the time of his death constitutes his "estate". Real property is land and anything attached to it; personal property is any tangible or intangible property such as personal effects, furniture, automobiles, jewelry, money, stocks, bonds, insurance proceeds payable to the estate, and the like.

As a rule, the estate is primarily responsible to pay the reasonable and necessary expenses of the disposition of the body. If the estate has property, the funeral director may look to it for payment of the funeral bill. The funeral bill will usually be accorded a high priority in the list of claims to be paid. In the probate law of most states there is a priority list of how the estate's debts will be paid. The funeral bill, or at least a substantial portion of the bill, is typically the second or third debt to be paid.

A good example of a priority list is found in Section 2117.25 of the Ohio Revised Code. Funeral expenses up to $4,000 and cemetery expenses up to $3,000 are listed in the second priority of the debts to be paid by an estate. That portion of the funeral bill in excess of $4,000 but less than $6,000 is given the sixth priority on the list of debts to be paid. Any part of the funeral bill in excess of $6,000 falls under the general debt category which is paid before bequests are made to heirs and legatees under the estate.

b. Reasonableness of the Funeral Bill.

If the decedent leaves a will that authorizes payment of funeral expenses, such provision is enforceable against the estate if it has sufficient assets to pay the bill. If the decedent does not leave a will, or if the will does not specifically provide for the payment of funeral expenses, the amount of funeral expenses properly charged against the estate will, in the absence of a statutory provision, be limited by the probate court to a reasonable amount.

If the court finds that the funeral bill is unreasonably high, it will not permit assets of the estate to be used to pay that amount which it finds to be unreasonable. In determining the reasonableness of a funeral bill, the courts will look at the following factors: (1) the size and solvency of the estate; (2) the right of the creditors; (3) the station in life of the decedent; (4) the decedent's religious faith; (5) the decedent's fraternal memberships; (6) local and contemporary custom; and (7) the funeral director's knowledge of the financial condition of the decedent.

The reasonableness of the funeral bill is often measured in relation to the size of the estate. For example, in *Succession of Smith*, 330 So.2d 402 (La.App. 1976), the court held that funeral charges amounting to $4,599 charged against an estate worth $26,500, although bordering on the excessive, were not out of proportion with the value of the estate.

The court must also weigh the station in life to which the decedent belonged. If the decedent maintained a higher position in life, a more expensive funeral may be justified. Likewise, if the local, ethical or religious customs to which the decedent adhered to require a more elaborate funeral, the court will be more inclined to permit a more expensive bill. Finally, the court may look at the knowledge of the funeral director. If the funeral director contracts for a pretentious funeral although he knows the estate is modest, the court will be less willing to permit the estate to pay the expensive funeral bill. On the other hand, if the funeral director had no knowledge that the estate was small, a court will be more inclined to approve a higher funeral bill.

c. Collection Against an Estate.

One of the principal disadvantages of looking to the estate for payment of the funeral bill is the delay in collection. Probate of an estate can often take up to a year after the death of the decedent. While probate laws in most states permit executors to pay funeral expenses from the estate even before the executor is appointed by the court, funeral directors in many cases encounter problems in promptly collecting funeral bills from estates. For these reasons, it is advisable for funeral directors to have additional parties execute the funeral contract. This enables the funeral director to collect the funeral bill from third parties if the estate delays in the payment of the bill.

6.3 Liability for Funeral Expenses of Dependent

The common law rule is that a husband and father are primarily liable to pay the funeral expenses of the wife and dependent children. This is true regardless of whether the wife or child leaves an estate or whether the husband or father signs the funeral contract. Moreover, the husband or father cannot recoup the funeral expenses from the decedent's estate. In other words, the husband or father is primarily liable and the estate is secondarily liable for the funeral expenses.

Because the common law rule has been superseded in some states by statutes making the estate primarily liable for funeral expenses, it is necessary for each funeral director to be aware of his or her own state laws. In addition, if the wife or child specifically provides in her or his will that the estate is to pay for the funeral, the husband or father's duty to pay the expenses is superseded by the estate. Finally, it should be noted that if another member of the family or a third party executes the funeral contract and agrees to become primarily liable to pay for it, the husband or father's obligation is extinguished.

Under the common law, the duty of the husband is not affected by the fact that the husband and wife are separated at the time of her death. Nor is his liability avoided by the fact that he did not arrange the funeral, that he did not attend it, or even that he was not aware of her death.

In general, under the common law there is no duty on the wife to pay for her husband's funeral. However, in some jurisdictions an exception to this rule is recognized where the husband's estate is inadequate to pay for the expenses. In addition, in some states there are statutes making a wife equally chargeable for family expenses, thereby abrogating the common law and making her responsible for the husband's funeral expenses.

For example, in *Davis-Turner Funeral Home, Inc. v. Chaney*, 61 O.Misc.2d 76 (1991), a widow, who refused to pay for her husband's funeral, was compelled to reimburse her stepson who paid for the funeral. The court held that under Ohio law a wife is statutorily obligated to pay for the funeral expenses of her husband when the estate is insolvent.

6.4 Contractual Liability

The person who requests a funeral director to undertake a funeral does not automatically make himself liable for the funeral expenses. Unless the law implies liability on his part because of his legal relation to the decedent or because he expressly or implicitly agrees to become individually liable for the funeral expense, he will not be responsible for the funeral bill. In some jurisdictions, a widow will become personally liable for the funeral expenses merely by the fact that she requests or orders the funeral arrangements. Cases from these jurisdictions hold that in the absence of a special understanding that the funeral home is to look to the estate for payment, the widow who arranges the funeral will be liable. Of course, this rule does not apply in those states wherein the statutory law makes the estate primarily liable.

Although an unrelated third party is not liable for funeral expenses even if he arranges the funeral, he can agree by oral or written contract to make himself personally liable to pay the funeral expenses. If a third party or a relative agrees to become personally liable on the contract, the funeral director should have the party execute a written contract. Moreover, in those cases where there is a question about the size or solvency of the estate, it is prudent for the funeral director to have a relative or third party become liable on the contract in the event the estate is unable to pay the funeral expenses.

6.5   Liability of Executor or Administrator

Usually the executor or administrator of the decedent's estate is not appointed until well after funeral services have been provided. Therefore, the question of his liability seldom arises. In those cases where the executor or administrator engages the service of the funeral director for the decedent, he may be personally bound to pay the funeral expenses unless he has stipulated against personal liability, or the circumstances are such as to clearly show that the funeral director was looking to the estate for primary payment. If an executor or administrator pays for the funeral from his own funds, he may be reimbursed by the estate for the reasonable expense of the funeral.

In *Davis-Turner Funeral Home, Inc. v. Chaney, supra*, the son had been appointed as executor for his father's estate. However, in signing the funeral contract, he had not stipulated that he was signing as the executor of the estate. Therefore, he was personally responsible for paying the bill. Fortunately for the son, the court found that the funeral expenses were ultimately the responsibility of the surviving spouse and ordered her to reimburse the son for those expenses.

Where an executor is vested by a will with authority to expend for funeral expenses such amount as he deems proper, the exercise of his discretion will not be reviewed by the probate court in the absence of a showing that he arbitrarily and improperly determined the amount to be expended for funeral expenses.

6.6   Liability of State

Where a funeral is ordered by a public official in the performance of the duties of his office, the state or one of its subdivisions may be rendered liable to the funeral director for the funeral. Of course, before agreeing to perform such a funeral, the funeral director should ensure that the state or one of its subdivisions will accept responsibility for payment of the bill.

State and local governments may also be responsible by law for the full or partial payment of indigent funerals. As states and municipalities have faced tightening budgets, funding for dispositions of indigents has been eliminated or restricted in many jurisdictions. Funeral directors need to know what government agencies make funds available for indigent funerals and how to make claims for those funds.

Chapter Seven

CREMATION

7.1   Overview

The level of cremation in the United States has continued at a steady growth rate for the past twenty years. The cremation rate in the U.S. in 2009 was 36% and experts predict that the rate will increase to 46% by the year 2015. Factors which have led to the increase include a growing acceptance by the public of cremation, the relocation of the elderly to Florida, Arizona, and other areas in the sunbelt, the influx of immigrants from cultures that prefer cremation, a higher level of education in the American public, environmental concerns and recent recessionary woes.

In response to this marketing trend, many funeral directors are expanding the goods and services they offer to families that desire cremation. Innovative funeral directors understand that cremation can often be part of a meaningful funeral experience. Cremation opens up new options and services for the family and the funeral director.

As well as increasing options, cremation also greatly increases the potential legal liability of funeral directors. Because cremation is an irreversible process, mistakes made by funeral directors often cannot be undone. This irreparable nature of cremation is the underlying reason why funeral directors must be extremely cautious in conducting business in this area.

In recent years, a rash of cremation liability lawsuits has alerted the funeral industry to the necessity of precautions in arranging and handling cremation. The Tri-State Crematory scandal in Noble, Georgia in 2002 also generated increased state regulation of cremation and crematories.

7.2   Authorization to Cremate

One of the keys to protecting the funeral home from liability is to utilize a detailed cremation authorization form. The purpose of the form is to document in writing the consent to the cremation, the authority of the agent authorizing the cremation, the identity of the decedent and information on medical devices, personal effects and the ultimate disposition of the cremated remains.

The genesis of the cremation authorization form used by most funeral homes is the model cremation law drafted by the Cremation Association of North America (CANA) in the mid-1980s. That law, which has been adopted in one form or another by a majority of the states, requires funeral homes and crematories to obtain detailed information from the authorizing agent in a written consent form. Among the most important provisions of the consent form are these:

(1) **Identification of the Decedent.** On the form, the funeral director lists basic information regarding the decedent including the name, address, place of death, date and time of death and social security number. In addition, there is a representation made by the authorizing agent that he or she has personally identified the decedent or has authorized his or her personal representative to identify the decedent at the funeral home. Personal identification by viewing the body is crucial to reducing liability in the event there is a misidentification.

(2) **Identification of Authorizing Agent.** The form also requires the agent who is authorizing the cremation to provide information such as name, address, and his or her relationship to the decedent.

(3) Authority of Authorizing Agent. On the cremation authorization form, the authorizing agent either represents that he or she has the paramount right to authorize the cremation or, if another person holds that right, the authorizing agent lists that person and certifies that the agent was unable to contact that person after trying to do so and has no reason to know that person would be opposed to the cremation.

(4) **Medical Devices.** The authorizing agent in the cremation authorization form will disclose whether there are any medical devices implanted in the body of the decedent and, if so, authorize their removal. This information is extremely important since certain implants, such as lithium powered pacemakers and defibrillators, may explode in the retort.

(5) **Authorization to Cremate, Process and Pulverize.** In the cremation authorization form, it is important to provide a detailed description of the cremation process. In order for the agent to provide informed consent to the cremation process, it is necessary for the agent to have a full explanation of what takes place in the cremation process, including the pulverization of the cremated remains.

(6) **Disposition of Personal Property.** To avoid liability, it is important for funeral directors to receive information as to what is to remain on the body during cremation and what disposition is to take place of items removed from the body prior to cremation. Examples include jewelry, clothes, hair pieces, eyeglasses, etc.

(7) **Instructions of Final Disposition.** One of the more significant areas of liability concerns the misdelivery of cremated remains. It is vital that the funeral director receive definitive instructions from the authorizing agent as to the ultimate disposition of the cremated remains. If they are to be shipped, the funeral director should obtain permission to ship them by a delivery service that has internal tracing capabilities and requires a written receipt from the recipient.

(8) **Authority to Dispose of Unclaimed Cremains.** With the increase in cremation, there has also been an increase in the number of unclaimed cremated remains held by funeral homes. To deal with this problem, many crema-

tion authorization forms contain a provision which authorizes the funeral director to lawfully dispose of the cremated remains if they are not claimed by the authorizing agent or his or her designee within a specified time period. Over two-thirds of the states have a law that authorizes the disposition of unclaimed cremated remains if they are not retrieved within a certain period. The period may be anywhere from 60 days to one year. It is important to check the applicable state law prior to disposing of any unclaimed cremated remains.

(9) **Recycling Metal.** With so many Americans undergoing joint replacements or having some type of medical implant, it is very common for those parts and implants to be removed from the retort after cremation. Many of these parts and implants contain valuable metals or ceramics which can be recycled. Funeral homes and crematories that intend to recycle metals or other materials must always receive written consent from the authorizing agent to retrieve the materials and recycle them. Is is also important to insure that recycling is permitted by state law.

(10) **Certification and Indemnification.** The cremation authorization form should contain a provision by which the authorizing agent certifies the accuracy of all statements on the form. In addition, the authorizing agent should indemnify the funeral director from any liability in the event any of the information on the cremation authorization form is incorrect. Many of the cremation authorization laws adopted by the states provide funeral directors with immunity from lawsuits if they rely in good faith upon the information provided to them by the authorizing agent in the cremation authorization form.

7.3   Other Cremation Forms

In addition to using a comprehensive cremation authorization form, funeral homes also need to document other events and decisions throughout the entire cremation process. When the body is delivered to a crematory, a receipt form should document the transfer of possession. Similarly, when the funeral home obtains the cremated remains from the crematory and returns the cremated remains to the authorizing agent, written receipts should be filled out and signed.

If there is any change in the method of disposition after the cremation authorization form is signed, it should be documented. If the authorizing agent wishes the cremated remains shipped or scattered by the funeral home, those decisions should be documented in a form. Likewise, any decision to commingle cremated remains should be detailed and authorized in a written form. Because many decisions in the cremation process are irreversible, documentation is an absolute necessity throughout the cremation process.

7.4   Investigating Third Party Crematories

It is clear that funeral homes that operate a crematory will be responsible for any wrongdoing or omission at the crematory. However, even for those funeral homes not operating a crematory, liability for crematory wrongdoings may be imputed to the funeral home. Because the funeral home often contracts with the crematory and because of the funeral home's overall supervisory responsibility in caring for the body, some courts have allowed families to sue funeral homes for the misdeeds of independent crematories.

To protect itself from liability for the acts or omissions of third party crematories, the funeral home should be able to demonstrate that it routinely investigates and checks the policies and procedures of the crematory and its method of operation. Then, if the crematory commits a wrongful act that harms a family that the funeral home is serving, the funeral home may be able to defend itself against a lawsuit by showing that it was not careless in retaining the third party crematory to perform cremations for the funeral home. This due diligence investigation of the third party crematory by the funeral home usually involves the three components listed below.

a. *Crematory Records Request*

At least once a year, the funeral home should request and obtain from the crematory copies of the following items:

- State crematory license or permit.
- Policy and procedure manual for crematory.
- Membership certificates from CANA, Better Business Bureau, or other organizations.
- List of crematory operators employed by the crematory and a copy of any operator certification.
- Copies of liability insurance policies and professional liability insurance policies carried by crematory.
- Copies of cremation authorizations, releases, and receipt forms used by the crematory.
- Copies of any state inspection reports to the crematory.
- Copies of the most recent maintenance/inspection reports or logs used internally by the crematory for its equipment.

These items should be received and reviewed to insure that the crematory is in compliance with state licensing laws and is utilizing proper procedures in carrying out cremation.

b. *Interview of Crematory Management*

The second step of crematory due diligence is to interview the management of the crematory to obtain information on its personnel, facilities and operation. Funeral home personnel conducting the interview should take written notes of the interview. If any response from the crematory is unsatisfactory or raises concerns, the funeral home should address the issue with the crematory manager immediately.

Topics covered by the interview typically include information on who owns the crematory, what experience does the current ownership have in running the crematory, how many employees does the crematory have, what experience and training is required of operators and who conducts the training. The interviewer should also obtain information on the crematory's retort, processing and refrigeration equipment, their age and condition, and service schedule. The final topic in the interview would cover operations of the crematory including a detailed explanation of all steps taken by the crematory from the time the body is received until the time that the cremated remains are delivered by the crematory.

c. Crematory Inspection

The last and most important component of the due diligence process is to conduct an unannounced inspection of the crematory during normal business hours. Funeral home personnel conducting the inspection should use a checklist to document their findings. If any problems are observed during the inspection, funeral home personnel should note them on the checklist, raise those concerns in writing to the management of the crematory, and make sure that the problems are remedied.

The checklist utilized by the funeral home personnel conducting the inspection would include items that the inspector would observe during a walk through of the crematory. Those items may include whether the crematory has posted its licenses and permits, whether operators are dressed appropriately and conducting business in a professional manner, whether the facilities are neat, clean and orderly, whether human remains awaiting cremation are held in a dignified and clean holding area, the operational condition of the retort, processing and refrigeration equipment, and whether the crematory maintains a crematory log that is up to date and an up to date equipment maintenance schedule.

Chapter Eight

DISINTERMENT

8.1   Disinterment Defined

Disinterment, or exhumation as it is sometimes called, may be defined as the removal of a dead body or remains from its place of repose after disposition has been completed. In the case of a burial, it means digging up and removal of the remains; in the case of cremation, it refers to the removal of cremated remains from their repository.

8.2   Disinterment Disfavored

In most jurisdictions, there is a strong public policy against disinterment. Many judicial decisions indicate that disinterment is not a matter of right and that ordinarily a court will not order or permit a body to be disinterred unless there is a strong showing that it is necessary and that the interest of justice requires the disinterment. Even the individual with the paramount right of disposition cannot disinter the body against the will of other relatives except upon strong and convincing evidence that persuades a court of equity that the disinterment is required by justice.

Many of the cases indicate that the law in principle abhors disinterment out of respect for the human desire not to have one's remains disturbed, the sentiment of survivors and the protection of public health. Therefore, disinterment is allowable only in cases where good cause for it is shown by the parties seeking to disinter a body.

Disinterment may be authorized by law on two principal grounds, either in the public interest or for private purposes. In the former, the public purpose may be to further some matter of public interest although the immediate reason may be private. In the latter, the purpose is purely private.

8.3   Disinterment in the Public Interest

Exhumations in the public interest usually involve the disinterment of the body and its reinterment in the same place. In such cases, the exhumation is normally made for evidentiary purposes, either for criminal or civil cases.

It is well-established that the state has the power to seek an exhumation for the purposes of gathering evidence for a criminal trial. Courts will readily grant enforcement officers the authority to exhume bodies if required for criminal investigations or trials.

In some cases, a party may seek to affirm or disaffirm an alleged cause of death in connection with an insurance policy. In these cases, exhumation for evidentiary purposes is permitted on the grounds that the possible existence of fraud should not be protected by the rule forbidding the disturbance of the repose of the dead. However, in civil cases such as these, a stronger burden of proof is usually required by the parties seeking disinterment than is required in criminal cases. For example, in *Application of Coleman*, 153 NYS 2d 936, a court denied the request of the decedent's sister to have the decedent's body disinterred for purposes of examination to ascertain the cause of death. Although the sister suspected foul play, the court noted that there had been an autopsy prior to burial, that the sister's suspicions were based on hearsay and on statements not under oath, and that there was nothing in the sister's application to indicate that public officials had failed to properly determine the cause of death.

Disinterment of a body and its reinterment in a different place may be made in the public interest to provide access for public streets. Bodies have also been disinterred in the public interest where they may constitute a threat to public health, such as the possibility of contaminating well water.

8.4 Disinterment for Private Purpose.

Exhumation for private purposes generally involves disinterment and reinterment at another place. There can be many reasons for private parties to seek disinterment. For example, the surviving spouse or next of kin may be dissatisfied with the place of interment. Oftentimes, due to the relocation of the family and a desire to be close to the place of interment, a family may seek to move the body to a cemetery within their locale. Bodies have sometimes been mistakenly interred in cemetery lots not owned by the family. In other cases, cemeteries have been abandoned or in such disrepair that the court will allow disinterment.

In many states, disinterment is a matter of statutory regulation. The usual procedure requires the surviving spouse and/or next of kin to make a written application to the trustees of the cemetery. A funeral director is usually required to be in attendance during this disinterment. Restrictions may be placed upon disinterment by the state for public health reasons.

Where no statutes govern the procedure, case law is controlling. Any interested party may make an application to a court of equity which then determines whether to grant the application for disinterment. Generally, the surviving spouse and/or the next of kin have the primary right to seek disinterment.

In determining whether there is good cause to order a disinterment, courts have indicated that each case must turn on its own particular facts. Nevertheless, when deciding whether reasonable cause exists for disinterment, courts have looked at the following factors: (1) the degree of the relationship that the party seeking disinterment bears to the decedent; (2) the degree of the relationship that the party seeking to prevent disinterment bears to the decedent; (3) the express wishes of the decedent; (4) the conduct of persons seeking disinterment, especially as it may relate to circumstances of the original interment; (5) the conduct of persons seeking to prevent disinterment; (6) the length of time that has elapsed since the original interment; (7) the strength of reasons offered both in favor and opposition to disinterment; (8) the integrity and compassion of persons seeking disinterment to provide a secure and comparable resting place for the decedent; and (9) the rights and principles of the religious body or other institution which granted the right to inter the body at the first place of burial.

Often a court will have to balance competing interests and make a choice based upon the judge's determination as to the importance of each factor. For example, in *Guerin v. Cassidy*, 38 N.J. 454, 119 A.2d 780 (1955), the decedent, a Catholic, was buried in a Catholic cemetery. Later when her will was discovered, the executor petitioned the court to allow removal to another Catholic cemetery which the decedent had named in her will. After balancing factors involved in the case, the court refused permission to disinter, finding as follows:

> "Although it may be recognized that the wishes or directions of the deceased as to his interment are entitled to respectful consideration and are allowed great weight, such directions, even though contained in a will, are not considered testamentary in nature, since there is no property right in a dead body in the ordinary sense. After interment, a body is in the custody of the law and removal is subject to the jurisdiction of this court. Such power, however, should not be exercised unless it is clearly shown that good cause and urgent necessity for such action exists.

> In light of the fact that the decedent is already buried in ground which, according to ecclesiastical law and the doctrine of her church, is consecrated and hallowed, and the cost incident to the removal to another cemetery would be excessive when compared to the size of the estate, there appears to be no good cause or urgent necessity to direct such removal."

Although religious law may be evidence to show the customs and wishes of those who observe its mandates, it is not binding on the court. In T*amarkin v. Children of Israel, Inc.*, 2 O. App. 2d 60 (1965) the defendant, an Orthodox Jewish cemetery, sought to prevent the decedent's next of kin from removing the decedent's remains to a Reformed Jewish Cemetery. The court held that the restriction in the cemetery deed prohibiting removal was in conflict with the statutory right of the next of kin to seek disinterment. The court therefore permitted the removal on the basis that a private contract grounded in ecclesiastical law cannot nullify an existing statute.

Oftentimes courts are called upon to settle family disputes regarding disinterment. In *Mallen v. Mallen*, 520 S.W. 2d 736 (Tenn. 1974), a widow sought to have her husband's remains removed from her in-laws' property.

The evidence showed that the parents of the decedent and the wife were very hostile to each other.

The court stated that there were a number of factors involved in the decision. First, the court noted that the parties were Jewish and that Jewish custom did not favor disinterment. The court also recognized the judicial principle that courts do not ordinarily permit disinterment unless there is a compelling reason to justify it.

However, the court noted that in this case there was no record of what the preferences of the decedent were. When there has been no request or express wish on the part of the decedent and there arises a conflict among the spouse and blood relations, the court found that the wishes of the spouse should command first consideration. In that respect, the court ruled as follows:

> "In past cases, many justifications have permitted disinterment by a surviving spouse. A few which might be mentioned are the fulfillment of the surviving spouse's expectation, where it was understood that the original interment was to only be temporary; the obtainment of side-by-side burial plots; reinterment in a location more accessible to the spouse; and reinterment in a location removed from family hostility."

Balancing the factors, the court allowed the wife to disinter the body and relocate it to another cemetery.

It is apparent that there are many diverse reasons for seeking disinterment and that it is impossible to judge the validity of them in advance of a decision by the court. Like many other situations encountered in the field of mortuary law, these cases each stand upon their own merits. If a funeral director has any doubts as to the proper authorization for disinterment, he should not participate in such disinterment until he has been assured that it has been legally authorized.

8.5 Unauthorized Disinterments

It is an indictable offense under statute and common law to disinter a dead body without proper authority regardless of the purpose or motive. It was held in the case of *State of North Carolina v. McLean*, 121 N.C. 589 (1897), that the members of a Board of Commissioners who opened graves in a town cemetery for the purpose of removing bodies for reburial in the free section of the cemetery because the original graves were unpaid for were guilty of a statute forbidding disinterment except with the consent of a surviving spouse or next of kin.

Chapter Nine

FUNERAL HOMES

9.1 Defined

A funeral home is a fixed place for the conducting of funerals and/or for the care and preparation of the dead prior to disposition. The determination of whether an establishment constitutes a funeral home will depend upon the activities carried on at that place. Generally, if dead bodies are taken to the establishment for preparation prior to burial or other disposition, or if funerals are conducted at the establishment (other than a religious establishment or public hall), the building will be considered a funeral home.

9.2 Licensing and Regulation

Just as the police power of state and local governments authorizes the licensing and regulation of funeral directors, it also permits the licensing and regulation of funeral homes. In most states there are comprehensive laws and administrative regulations governing the operation of funeral homes. Funeral homes are subject to inspection by government agencies to insure hygiene, health and safety. Moreover, as seen in Chapter Thirteen, funeral homes are increasingly under the scrutiny of the Occupational Safety and Health Administration, the federal agency responsible for safe working conditions.

With regard to licensing, courts have routinely upheld restrictions that state governments have placed on who may operate a funeral home. For example, a Pennsylvania law allowing professional or restricted corporations to establish branch funeral homes, but denying business corporations that privilege, was upheld in *H.B. Brandt Funeral Home, Inc. v. Commonwealth*, 78 Pa. Cmwlth. 206, 467 A.2d 106 (1983). The court ruled that the law served a legitimate state goal of protecting the public. The court reasoned that since professional and restricted corporations were owned by licensed funeral directors and their families, the legislature could reasonably assume that these operations would conduct their businesses in accordance with the highest standards of the funeral profession. However, since business corporations could be owned by non-licensed shareholders, the profit motives of the shareholders could influence the funeral home's operation so that it was not conducted in accordance with the standards of funeral homes owned by professional or restricted corporations.

Maryland, like Pennsylvania, restricts funeral home ownership to licensed funeral directors. When Maryland's law was challenged in the case of *Brown v. Hovetter*, 561 F.3d 357 (4th Cir. 2009), the state argued that the law promoted familiarity between the owner and his business. The court accepted that as a valid reason and cited the lower court's finding that ownership may be limited in highly skilled occupations where licensing is required, such as mortuary science. The court found that the licensing restriction was justified by "very real benefits of protecting the public health, safety, and welfare by encouraging familiarity of the owner of a funeral business with the day-to-day workings of that business and creating accountability to regulators and to clients."

While courts will routinely uphold laws restricting funeral home operations that have any rational relationship to public health or safety, courts tend to examine administrative regulations of state boards with greater scrutiny. For example, in *Labach v. Board of Embalmers and Funeral Directors*, 12 N.J. Super 334, 79 A.2d 693 (1951), the court rejected a rule of the State Board that prohibited a funeral director from serving as a manager of more than one funeral home. The court held that the regulation did not have any reasonable relationship to the safeguarding of the public health. Similarly, in *Golubski v. Board of Embalmers*, 114 O. App. 111, 180 N.E.2d 861 (1961), the court found that the State Board could not prohibit the serving of food or intoxicating liquor in conjunction with a funeral since such powers exceeded the Board's statutory authority.

9.3 Location of Funeral Homes

a. Nuisance

Under the common law, a nuisance is an invasion of a landowner's interest in the reasonable use and enjoyment of his land. Put differently, a nuisance is an unreasonable, unusual, or unnatural use of one's property so that it disturbs the peaceful, quiet and undisturbed use and enjoyment of nearby property.

In communities where the location of funeral homes is not governed by zoning laws or other regulation, funeral homes have sometimes been the target of nuisance actions brought by adjoining landowners. Typically, these suits have alleged that the presence of the funeral home causes psychological depression to neighbors as well as depreciation in property values.

Recognizing that funeral homes are lawful and necessary businesses for the public health and safety, courts have generally refused to declare that funeral homes are nuisances. However, in some cases where funeral homes are located in an area that is strictly or predominantly residential in nature, funeral homes have been found to be a nuisance. For example, in *Higgins v. Bloch*, 213 Ala. 209, 104 So. 429 (1925), the court held that the proposed establishment of a funeral home in a long-standing residential neighborhood would constitute a nuisance in that it would depreciate property values and inconvenience, disturb, and depress neighboring homeowners.

Nuisance suits have not fared well when the funeral home is located in a business area or an area in transition. In *Potter v. Bryan Funeral Home*, 307 Ark. 142, 817 S.W. 2d 882 (1991), property owners sought to stop a funeral home by arguing that it would depress property values. The court dismissed this suit noting that there were four or five other businesses within two blocks of the proposed funeral home. Therefore, when the area in question is a mix of commercial and residential uses, nuisance suits generally will not prevail.

b. Zoning Regulations

As part of its police power, municipalities have the general authority to adopt zoning ordinances. A zoning ordinance is a regulation dividing the municipality into geographical sections and specifying for each such section the nature, character and use of buildings or occupancy within that section. For example, the zoning plan may designate a certain area as "residential", thereby precluding the establishment of business enterprises in that particular area.

Although many older funeral home buildings in this country may have at one time served as residences, it is well-recognized that a funeral home is a commercial use or business use of property, and not a residential use. It therefore follows that a funeral home may not be established in a residential area since it constitutes a business. On the other hand, since funeral homes are a legitimate business use of property, they may be established in most areas zoned for commercial use. This offers the funeral home protection against objecting neighbors. For example, when neighbors challenged a funeral home as a nuisance in *Linsler v. Booth Undertaking Company*, 120 Wash. 177, 206 P. 676 (1922), the court dismissed the suit noting that the funeral home was located in a district zoned for business use. The zoning ordinance shielded the funeral home from the nuisance claim.

While funeral homes generally cannot be operated in an area zoned for residential use, there are certain exceptions. If a municipality adopts a new zoning ordinance or changes an existing ordinance, it will often "grandfather" existing non-conforming uses. For example, if a funeral home was already operating in an area that a new zoning ordinance designates as residential, the law may permit the property to be maintained as a funeral home even though it does not conform to the new zoning use. While this allows the funeral home to continue, it may restrict any expansion, renovation or rebuilding of the current structure. Moreover, once the funeral home operation ceases in that building, it can no longer be used as a funeral home.

When establishing residential areas by zoning regulations, a municipality may permit professional offices to be operated out of a residence. In cases where a doctor, dentist, musician or other professional lives in the residence, he or she has been permitted to operate an office out of the house. Most jurisdictions that permit such office use by professionals have ruled that funeral directing is not a profession that qualifies for this exception. The prevailing view by courts is that the occupation of a funeral director is a business and not a profession.

Residential zoning ordinances have also occasionally permitted places of assembly or public or quasi-public buildings to be maintained in a residential area. Generally, these exceptions are enacted to permit theaters or other places of amusement in neighborhoods. Most courts have ruled that funeral homes do not qualify as either a place of assembly or a public building, and therefore, this exception is not available to funeral homes.

Another zoning problem that can arise for funeral homes concerns the construction of a retort in a funeral home. If the funeral home is in a residential area, there will often be opposition from neighbors. Some funeral homes have been able to successfully argue that the crematory retort is an "accessory use" to the funeral home.

Most zoning laws will permit the property owner to construct buildings on the property which are consistent with the principal use of the property. These "accessory uses" are uses of land that are found on the same parcel as the principal use but are subordinate or incidental to the principal use. A classic example is a detached garage which is an accessory use to a residence. In several court cases, courts have found that retorts are accessory uses to funeral homes and have allowed them to be constructed on funeral home property.

c. *Conclusion*

It is generally very difficult to establish a new funeral home in a residential area. Because of restrictive zoning laws or the possibility of a nuisance suit, most funeral homes are now located in strictly commercial areas or areas that permit joint use by businesses and residences. Of course, because of grandfathering provisions in zoning ordinances, there are still many funeral homes operating in predominantly residential areas across the country.

Obviously, a funeral director planning to build a funeral home or to convert an existing building into a funeral home must carefully research existing zoning laws in the municipality to determine if such property use is permissible. If no zoning ordinances are in place, an evaluation of the area should be made to ascertain if neighboring landowners will object to the funeral home. The assistance of a real estate attorney with expertise in zoning matters is usually recommended.

9.4   Licensing of Other Death Care Facilities

Businesses and individuals other than licensed funeral homes and funeral directors are increasingly offering death care services. For example, in about fifteen states, direct disposition companies and crematories that are not licensed as funeral homes may lawfully offer their services directly to the public. Shipping services, removal and livery services, embalming facilities, and refrigeration and storage facilities, many of which offer their services to funeral homes and in some cases to the public, have also sprung up in many states.

In response to these emerging businesses, especially the increase in the number of crematories, states have begun to update and expand their licensing statutes and regulations. For example, in the wake of the Tri-State Crematory scandal in Noble, Georgia, ten states enacted new or expanded crematory licensing laws in 2002. States have also adopted new laws and regulations requiring registration of livery and removal services, embalming facilities and refrigeration and storage. The State of Florida, where cremations and ship-outs are commonplace, provides an excellent example of comprehensive licensing laws for crematories, refrigeration and storage facilities, and removal services.

9.5   Americans With Disabilities Act

a.   Overview

One of the principal purposes of the Americans With Disabilities Act is to provide disabled individuals with full use and enjoyment of public accommodations. The public accommodation related section of the ADA took effect on January 26, 1992. Generally, it requires businesses to remove architectural, communication and transportation barriers, provided that removal is "readily achievable", i.e. removal can be accomplished without much difficulty or expense taking into consideration the cost of the removal as well as the size and financial resources of the business.

Since funeral homes are defined as public accommodations, they are subject to this section of the ADA. The ADA has two sets of standards for public accommodations. The more stringent standards are for those buildings or additions that were occupied after January, 1993. Since the law was enacted in July, 1990, any new building that was constructed for occupancy after January, 1993 should have been designed to fully comply with the ADA stringent standards.

For older buildings that existed prior to January, 1993, the ADA prescribes a more relaxed standard. However, as seen below, this standard may require funeral homes to make substantial investments in order to be in compliance with the ADA.

b.   Priorities

In undertaking the process of removing barriers to disabled individuals, the ADA sets out a priority list for owners of public accommodations. The first priority is for the owner to provide access to the facility from public sidewalks, parking facilities and public transportations. Therefore, the owner's first priority should be to erect permanent ramps, widen entrance doorways, make curb cuts and designate disabled parking areas.

The second priority for the building owner is to provide access to areas of the public accommodation where goods or services are made available to the public. For example, the funeral director should insure access to chapels and visitation areas, arrangement offices and casket sales areas. Assistive listening devices should be installed in chapels. Furniture should be rearranged to permit sufficient space in aisles for access by wheelchairs, and shelves and other displays should be repositioned so that sale items can be displayed to those who are not standing.

The third priority is to establish access to restroom facilities. Doors and toilet stall areas should be widened, toilet seats raised, grab bars installed, paper towel dispensers lowered and full length mirrors installed.

The final priority is to take any other measures needed to insure access to goods, services and the facilities of the public accommodation. This would include repositioning public telephones, lowering drinking fountains, removing any high pile carpet which impedes access by wheelchair bound individuals, adding raised marking on elevator control buttons for sight impaired individuals, installing flashing alarm lights for hearing impaired individuals, and installing accessible door hardware.

c. Readily Achievable Test

Some of the barrier removals cited above can involve significant expense to the owner of the funeral home. It is important to note that all barrier removals are not necessarily required by the ADA. The ADA requires only those removables which are "readily achievable".

In determining if removal is readily achievable, the ADA directs the owner of the public accommodation to evaluate the following factors:

(1) the cost and nature of the removal;

(2) the overall financial resources of the business, the number of people employed at the site, the expense of instituting the removal, and the impact it will have on the operation of the business; and

(3) if there is a parent company, the overall resources of the parent. For example, a barrier removal that is not readily achievable for an independent funeral home may be readily achievable by a firm that is part of a large conglomerate.

In the first analysis, the owner of the public accommodation is the judge of what is readily achievable. The regulations promulgated under the ADA indicate that each case will be judged on its particular facts and weight will be accorded to the business judgment of the owner. However, if an owner's decision not to remove a barrier is challenged, the owner has the burden of proof in showing that the removal was not readily achievable.

If challenged, two factors will help the owner's defense. First, if the owner can show that the business engaged in a self assessment and made a deliberate decision not to remove a barrier, it will show a minimum good faith effort with compliance. The second factor which assists the owner's defense is to show that the owner instituted, or at least investigated, alternatives to the barrier removal. For example, if a funeral home has its casket display room on a second floor which is not accessible to wheelchair bound individuals, it would show good faith if the funeral home had assembled a binder containing photographs and detailed description of all its casket offerings for those individuals who did not have access to the casket display room.

d. Withholding of Services

The ADA protects not only disabled individuals but also anyone with a close relationship to the disabled individual. Therefore, family members of disabled individuals generally are within the protective scope of the ADA.

If an individual with AIDS or other contagious disease dies, a funeral home that refuses to embalm the body or offer funeral services has violated the ADA. The family members of that deceased disabled individual may bring an action under the ADA against the funeral home since AIDS cases may be safely embalmed by adhering to universal precautions.

If embalming does pose an undue hazard to the safety of the embalmer, the funeral home would be within its right under the ADA to refuse to embalm. An example might include a victim of CJD where the funeral home would not have the equipment nor the expertise to embalm without creating a risk of infection.

It is also important to note that in offering services to disabled individuals and their families, owners of public accommodations cannot impose surcharges for extra costs that may be imposed. In the case of funeral directors, contagious disease surcharges for embalming are prohibited by the ADA. Individual lawsuits and enforcement actions by the Department of Justice have been brought against funeral homes that impose surcharges when embalming individuals that have died of contagious disease.

Another area where the obligations of the ADA will impact funeral homes concerns individuals who are deaf and require interpreters to communicate. Because the ADA obligates businesses that provide services to the public to make reasonable accommodations so that those with disabilities can enjoy the benefit of those services, funeral homes that conduct visitations and funeral services must provide interpreters upon the request of a deaf attendee. Furthermore, the funeral home may not impose any cost or fee for doing so. Therefore, if requested by a deaf attendee, a funeral home must provide an interpreter at its own costs for services that it supervises, even those held outside of the funeral home facility.

e. Enforcement

The public accommodations section of the ADA may be enforced by either the U.S. Attorney General's office or private individuals. If a public accommodation is found to have violated the ADA, the court may order the business to remove a barrier and fine the business up to $50,000 for a first offense and $100,000 for subsequent violations. In addition, the court may award attorneys fees to a private plaintiff.

Chapter Ten

PRENEED FUNERAL CONTRACTS

10.1 In General

Preneed funeral contracts refer to contracts entered into between members of the public and funeral homes to provide for funeral goods and services in the future upon the death of the contract beneficiary. The purchaser of the preneed contract typically prefunds the contract either through a payment made to the funeral home at the time the contract is entered into or by the purchase of an insurance policy upon the life of the contract beneficiary. When the contract beneficiary dies, the funeral home carries out the terms of the contract and provides the promised funeral goods and services.

Preneed contracts may be guaranteed fixed price contracts or non-guaranteed. In the former case, the funeral home guarantees to the purchaser that the price of the funeral to be provided in the future will not exceed the amount of funds paid on the contract plus any accruals thereon. If the contract is not guaranteed, the funeral home is only agreeing that amounts paid on the contract, plus accruals, will be applied toward the price of the future funeral. In the event that the price of the future funeral exceeds the amounts set aside to pay for it, the purchaser or the decedent's estate will have to make up the balance.

Another variable found in preneed contracts is the issue of revocability. Preneed contracts which are revocable may be terminated by the purchaser at any time prior to the death of the beneficiary with the purchaser receiving a refund of all or some part of the funds paid on the contract, plus all or some of the accruals thereon. The amount that is returned is often determined by state law. If the contract is irrevocable, the purchaser may not cancel it. However, approximately two-thirds of the states allow the purchaser an unconditional right to transfer an irrevocable preneed contract to another funeral home.

Although preneed contracts have existed for many years, it is only in the past forty years that their use has been widespread. With many funeral homes now actively promoting preneed arrangements and with the emergence of national marketing programs sponsored by large insurance companies, funeral home chains and state funeral trade associations, the trend toward preneed has been explosive. It has been estimated that by the year 2015 funeral directors will be writing two and one-half million preneed contracts per year. Obviously, if this projection holds up, the number of preneed contracts written on an annual basis will soon surpass at-need contracts.

10.2 Preneed Funding by Trust

With the emergence of preneed funeral contracts, state legislatures became concerned with the opportunity for fraud that was inherent with these arrangements. Noting that the contractual obligations of the funeral director were often not performed for up to twenty years after they received payment, the legislatures enacted various provisions to ensure that sellers of preneed funeral contracts had sufficient funds in the future to fulfill their contractual obligations. Typically, these laws require the seller of preneed funeral contracts to place all or some part of the preneed funds in a trust. When the contract beneficiary died and the funeral services were provided, the preneed funds could be withdrawn and paid to the funeral home.

Preneed trust laws and/or regulations have now been enacted in all fifty states and the District of Columbia. Although the trend is toward requiring an amount less than 100% of the preneed funds and interest thereon to be trusted, approximately one-half of states still require that all preneed funds and the interest earned thereon must remain in trust until the death occurs. The laws also usually require the funds to be deposited in insured banks, trust companies, or savings and loan accounts. Some states permit funeral directors to commingle the preneed accounts into one master account so that greater returns can be realized.

While nearly one-half of the states require a business selling preneed funeral services to be a licensed funeral home, nearly every state allows businesses to sell funeral goods on a preneed basis without the necessity of having a funeral home license. Therefore, in most states the market is open to third party sellers, especially cemeteries which seek to sell caskets and vaults to consumers on a preneed basis. These sellers often use aggressive marketing programs such as direct mail, telesales and door-to-door solicitation to promote their preneed contract sales.

Because trusting laws, especially 100% trusting laws, deprive preneed sellers of available income, these laws have been attacked by third party sellers as unconstitutional deprivations of property and the right to contract. In addition, some state laws which limit or restrict door-to-door and other means of direct solicitation have been challenged as unconstitutional infringements on free speech.

For the most part, the courts have upheld the validity of state preneed laws as legitimate exercises of police power. For example, in *Memorial Gardens Assoc., Inc. v. Smith*, 16 Ill.2d 116, 156 N.E.2d 587 (1959), third party sellers challenged the 95% trusting requirements of the Illinois preneed statute. Noting that the average time lapse of 29 years between payment and performance invited fraud, the court upheld the law as a reasonable regulation enacted in the public interest. The same result was reached in *Messerli v. Monarch Memorial Gardens*, 397 P.2d 34 (Idaho 1964), where the court upheld a 100% trusting requirement. The decision held that the Idaho preneed law was not unconstitutional even if it did deprive legitimate businesses of operating funds since it was a reasonable measure taken pursuant to the state's power to prevent fraud and deceit.

Federal appellate courts have also upheld challenges to state licensing laws which require funeral directors to sell preneed funeral services. In *Guardian Plans Inc. v. Teague*, 870 F.2d 123 (4th Cir. 1989), the appellant argued that it was irrational for the state to require an individual to have the training and education required of a funeral director in order to simply sell preneed funeral services. The court refused to second guess the Virginia General Assembly's licensing law's requirement. It held that the legislature may have rationally determined that keeping the arrangements of funerals in the hands of licensed funeral directors would benefit the public by insuring competence in funeral arrangements. It therefore upheld the law.

With regard to First Amendment claims, a federal district court has upheld a West Virginia preneed law against claims that it violated the right of free speech. The law in question banned uninvited door-to-door and telephone solicitation of preneed funeral contracts. The court, noting past incidents of fraud and undue influence by third party sellers, held that the state had a significant governmental interest in protecting the public from improper solicitation practices. Since the ban only restricted the time, place and manner of speech and not the content of speech, and since the preneed sellers had ample alternative means of solicitation (direct mail, mass advertisement), the court found that the solicitation restrictions were rationally related to a legitimate state purpose. *National Funeral Services, Inc. v. Rockefeller*, (1986, U.S. District Court of Southern District of West Va., unreported).

10.3 Preneed Funding By Insurance

Burial insurance policies have been in existence for many years. This form of insurance, which was especially popular in the South, is payable in services or merchandise or as a credit toward services or merchandise. The insurance as usually in the form of a contract in which the purchaser is to be provided a funeral and the proceeds cannot be used otherwise.

Funeral insurance, on the other hand, is life insurance which is used to fund a separate preneed contract. It is typically a life insurance policy with the funeral home being designated as the beneficiary or the assignee of the policy. The growth of funeral insurance as a funding mechanism for preneed contracts has increased dramatically in recent times as large life insurance companies have established national preneed programs.

Preneed funding through insurance rather than trusting does offer two distinct advantages. Most preneed insurance products offer some type of face amount escalator which increases the insurance payoff to meet inflation. Unlike preneed trusts where interest or income earned by the trust is taxable, the accrual in the face amount of the insurance policy is tax free. Not only does this result in tax savings, but it also relieves funeral directors and trustees of administrative costs.

The second primary advantage in funding through insurance is the receipt by the funeral home of upfront income to cover the cost of its preneed marketing program. Since in most cases the funeral director serves as the insurance agent, he or she is usually able to obtain a commission upon the execution of the policy. Unlike those situations where a funeral home has to trust 100% of the funds until a future date, this feature of insurance preneed funding provides the funeral home with immediate compensation to help meet the cost of operating a preneed program.

In every state, life insurance must only be sold through a licensed life insurance agent. In most states a funeral director may obtain such a license. However, a few states prohibit a funeral director from becoming a licensed insurance agent. Other states restrict the dollar amount of policies funeral directors may sell or provide that they may only sell policies, the proceeds of which are intended to be assigned as payment for preneed goods and services.

10.4 Taxation of Preneed Income

As stated earlier, accruals on preneed insurance policies are not taxed. However, interest or income paid on preneed trust funds deposited in banks or elsewhere is subject to federal income tax. Prior to 1987 there was a great uncertainty regarding who paid this tax: the funeral director, the purchaser of the preneed contract or the trustee of the preneed contract.

In late 1987, the Internal Revenue Service issued Revenue Ruling 87-127 to clarify the tax status of preneed trusts. That Ruling held that the consumer purchasing the preneed contract should pay the income tax on the interest earned by the preneed trust fund, regardless of whether the preneed contract was revocable or irrevocable. This ruling caused considerable consternation for some consumers who bristled at having to pay taxes on funds they would never receive.

As a result, Congress in 1997 enacted Section 685 to the IRS Code which allows a trustee to elect Qualified Fund Trust status (QFT). If a QFT election is made, the trust pays any tax rather than the consumer. QFTs originally had dollar limits that started at $7,000 and were indexed to inflation. In 2008, Congress eliminated the dollar ceilings on QFTs.

When the funeral services are performed and the funeral home receives the preneed funds in payment, these funds and all accruals thereon represent ordinary income to the funeral home. Likewise, if a funeral home is permitted by law to retain part of the preneed funeral payments or interest thereon prior to performing the service, these receipts of principal and interest will also be reported as ordinary income.

10.5 Medicaid/SSI

In determining eligibility for Medicaid assistance from the state or

Supplemental Security Income ("SSI") from the Social Security Administration, the government examines the resources and income of applicants. If those resources and income are below certain levels, the applicant is eligible for assistance. When determining the value of the applicant's resources, the Medicaid or SSI caseworker will exclude or not count certain assets. Preneed funeral funds may be viewed as one of the excludable assets if the preneed contract is properly constructed.

a. Irrevocable Preneed Funeral Contracts

Under current SSI and Medicaid regulations, all funds placed in a pre-need trust by a funeral home to fund an irrevocable preneed contract which are specifically identified to cover future funeral expenses are excluded from an applicant's resources. In most states, there is no dollar limitation on this exclusion. Therefore, SSI and Medicaid applicants who are purchasing pre-need funerals should be encouraged to enter into irrevocable preneed contracts so that the funds paid for the preneed arrangements will be excluded from their countable resources.

b. Burial Space Exclusion

In those states that prohibit or restrict the use of irrevocable preneed contracts, it still is possible to exclude all or part of the preneed funds from being counted as a resource. Current law provides a burial space exclusion that excludes the value of gravesites, crypts, mausoleums, urns, vaults, caskets or other repositories which are customarily and traditionally used for the remains of deceased persons from an applicant's resources. This exclusion applies in both revocable and irrevocable situations and it has no dollar limitation.

In order for the burial space exclusion to apply, the applicant must own the gravesite, casket, vault, etc. It is not, however, necessary that the applicant have physical possession of the burial space items. It is sufficient if the preneed contract shows the applicant's ownership of the burial space items. The contract should state that the applicant has purchased the particular burial space item and it should list the price of each such item. It is not necessary that the item be in existence at the time of the purchase as long as the purchase itself is evident from the contract.

c. Burial Funds Exclusion

In addition to the burial space exclusion, there is a burial fund exclusion which can exclude up to $1,500 that is designated to pay for funeral expenses. Funds set aside for burial include revocable burial contracts, burial trusts and separately identifiable assets which are clearly designated to cover expenses connected with the individual's burial, cremation or other funeral arrangements. This burial fund exclusion can be used to cover the cost of funeral services such as embalming, professional service fees, hearse costs, cremation fees, etc. which are not covered by the burial space exclusion.

If a revocable preneed contract is used, and the applicant wishes to exclude all of the preneed funds as a resource, it is necessary that the value of those items not covered by the unlimited burial space exclusion be no more than the $1,500 exclusion available under the burial fund exclusion. To the extent that these items exceed the $1,500 limitation, the excess will be counted as a resource of the applicant for Medicaid/SSI eligibility purposes.

10.6 FTC Door-to-Door Regulation

If a preneed sale takes place outside of the funeral establishment, it is very possible that the preneed sales activity is subject to the Federal Trade Commission's Cooling-Off Regulation for Door-to-Door Sales. This regulation mandates that all door-to-door sellers must notify their customers that they have the right to cancel the door-to-door transaction at any time prior to midnight of the third business day after the date of the transaction.

This regulation has a broad application because of the rather expansive definitions given the terms "door-to-door sales" and "consumer goods and services." A door-to-door sale is defined as a sale of consumer goods or services exceeding $25.00 in which the seller personally solicits the sale and the sale is made at a place other than the seller's place of business. This term applies regardless of whether the seller initiated the solicitation or whether he responded to the invitation of the buyer.

"Consumer goods and services" are any goods or services purchased, leased or rented primarily for personal, family or household purposes. According to the Federal Trade Commission, funeral transactions are included in this definition. Given these broad definitions, it is clear that preneed funeral sellers who conduct business away from their established place of business would be subject to the regulation.

There is one exception under the regulation which may exempt certain preneed funeral transactions from the regulation. The exemption applies if the door-to-door sales are made pursuant to prior negotiations which took place when the consumer visited a retail business establishment where the goods and services are offered for sale. For example, if a consumer visited the funeral establishment to make the initial contact and later the preneed arrangements were made at the consumer's home, the FTC's Door-to-Door Regulation would not apply. It should be noted that this exemption is only available if the initial negotiations are made pursuant to an in-person visit to the funeral establishment; a phone call is not sufficient.

If the regulation does apply to the preneed funeral transaction, the funeral director will be committing an unfair or deceptive act or practice if he does any of the following:

(a) Fails to provide the consumer with a copy of the contract, or if a contract does not exist, a receipt which is dated, contains the seller's name and address, and the following disclosure in 10 point bold-faced type:

"You, the Buyer, may cancel this transaction at any time prior to midnight of the third business day after the date of this transaction. See the attached notice of cancellation form for an explanation of this right."

On the contract, the above disclosure must be in close proximity to the signature line for the buyer. If a receipt is given, the disclosure must appear on the front of the receipt.

(b) Fails to furnish the consumer a fully completed copy of the Notice of Cancellation which must be attached to the contract or receipt and must be in 10 point bold-faced print. Seller must also retain a completed copy for himself. The Notice of Cancellation must be in the following form:

NOTICE OF CANCELLATION

(Date) _____

YOU MAY CANCEL THIS TRANSACTION WITHOUT ANY PENALTY OR OBLIGATION, WITHIN THREE BUSINESS DAYS FROM THE ABOVE DATE.

IF YOU CANCEL, ANY PROPERTY TRADED IN, ANY PAYMENTS MADE BY YOU UNDER THE CONTRACT OR SALE, AND ANY NEGOTIABLE INSTRUMENT EXECUTED BY YOU WILL BE RETURNED WITHIN TEN BUSINESS DAYS FOLLOWING RECEIPT BY THE SELLER OF YOUR CANCELLATION NOTICE, AND ANY SECURITY INTEREST ARISING OUT OF THE TRANSACTION WILL BE CANCELLED.

IF YOU CANCEL, YOU MUST MAKE AVAILABLE TO THE SELLER AT YOUR RESIDENCE, IN SUBSTANTIALLY AS GOOD CONDITION AS WHEN RECEIVED, ANY GOODS DELIVERED TO YOU UNDER THIS CONTRACT OR THE SALE; OR YOU MAY IF YOU WISH, COMPLY WITH THE INSTRUCTIONS OF THE SELLER REGARDING THE RETURN SHIPMENT OF THE GOODS AT THE SELLER'S EXPENSE AND RISK.

IF YOU DO MAKE THE GOODS AVAILABLE TO THE SELLER AND THE SELLER DOES NOT PICK THEM UP WITHIN TWENTY DAYS OF THE DATE OF YOUR NOTICE OF CANCELLATION, YOU MAY RETAIN OR DISPOSE OF THE GOODS WITHOUT ANY FURTHER OBLIGATION. IF YOU FAIL TO MAKE THE GOODS AVAILABLE TO THE SELLER, OR IF YOU AGREE TO RETURN THE GOODS TO THE SELLER AND FAIL TO DO SO, THEN YOU REMAIN LIABLE FOR PERFORMANCE OF ALL OBLIGATIONS UNDER THE CONTRACT.

TO CANCEL THIS TRANSACTION, MAIL OR DELIVER A SIGNED AND DATED COPY OF THIS CANCELLATION NOTICE OR ANY OTHER WRITTEN NOTICE OR SEND A TELEGRAM TO [name of seller] AT [address of seller's place of business] NO LATER THAN MIDNIGHT OF [date].

I HEREBY CANCEL THIS TRANSACTION.

(Date) _____

(Buyer's Signature) _____

(c) Includes in any door-to-door contract or receipt a confession of judgment or a waiver of the consumer's right of cancellation.

(d) Fails to orally inform the consumer about his right of cancellation or misrepresent that right in any way.

(e) Fails or refuses to honor a valid notice of cancellation. If a valid cancellation is received, all payments must be returned and all negotiable instruments signed by the buyer must be cancelled within ten business days after the notice of cancellation.

(f) Transfers, sells or assigns a negotiable instrument signed by the buyer to any third party within five business days of the transaction.

(g) Fails, within ten days of cancellation, to notify the buyer whether the seller intends to repossess any shipped goods.

Chapter Eleven

WAGE AND HOUR LAWS

11.1 Overview

The Fair Labor Standards Act ("FLSA") (29 USC §201 et seq.) covers three areas of employment law that are important to funeral service: minimum wage, overtime compensation, and equal pay.

11.2 Enforcement

The FLSA is administered and enforced by the Wage and Hour Division of the Department of Labor. The Wage and Hour Division's enforcement responsibilities are carried out by compliance officers stationed across the United States. These enforcement officers have the authority to conduct investigations and to gather data on wages, hours and other employment practices in order to determine compliance with the FLSA. Where violations are found, they may recommend changes in employment practices to bring an employer into compliance. Investigations may occur as a result of routine audits or on the basis of an employee complaint.

Willful violations of the Act may result in criminal prosecution by the Division. In addition to criminal actions, the Wage and Hour Division, as well as individual claimants, can institute a civil action in federal or state court for unpaid minimum wages or overtime pay. Funeral directors should be aware that it is a violation of the FLSA to terminate or in any way retaliate against an employee for filing a complaint or participating in an investigation of the Wage and Hour Division.

With regard to civil actions, a court may award unpaid wages and over-time pay for a back pay period of up to two years from the date the complaint is filed. In the case of a willful violation, the back pay period can extend to three years. A willful violation occurs when the employer willingly violates the Act or is in reckless disregard of it. In addition to back pay, the court can award private litigants their attorney fees. Finally, the court can award an additional amount as liquidated damages which is equal to the back pay amount. In other words, the court can double the back pay award.

11.3 Coverage under the FLSA

a. Employers

Not all employers are covered by the Act. Currently, an enterprise is fully covered if its gross annual sales exceed $500,000. For those funeral homes below the $500,000 gross revenue threshold, they still will be subject to overtime pay, child labor restrictions, and recordkeeping requirements if they grossed $362,000 or more in any year prior to 1990. For a funeral home, all proceeds from cash advances are included as part of gross receipts.

b. Employees

Full-time employees are generally protected by the overtime and minimum wage requirements of the FLSA unless they qualify under the so-called "white collar" exemptions. The five white collar exemptions are as follows:

(1) **Executive Employee.** In order to fall under the executive employee exemption, an employee's primary duty must consist of the management of the enterprise in which he is employed or of a customarily recognized department or subdivision of that enterprise. The employee must customarily and regularly direct the work of two or more other employees in the enterprise. Examples of executive employees in the funeral profession may include the general manager of the funeral home or a branch manager.

(2) **Administrators.** An employee can fall under the administrator exemption if his primary duty requires the exercise of discretion and independent judgment, and consists of the performance of office or non-manual work directly related to management policies or general business operations.

Generally, secretaries and clerical workers rarely fall under this exemption. Typically, an office manager or a personnel director would qualify for this exemption. The key determinant is whether the administrator has a wide degree of discretion in the performance of his job.

(3) **Professionals.** The standards for determining if an individual falls under the classification of a professional are as follows:

- The employee's primary duties consist of the performance of learned, artistic or educational matters requiring advance knowledge;
- The advance knowledge is customarily acquired by a prolonged course of specialized intellectual instruction;
- The employee's work requires the consistent exercise of discretion and judgment; and
- The employee's work is predominantly intellectual and varied in character and his output cannot be standardized in relationship to time.

(4) **Commissioned Outside Salesmen.** An employee who customarily and regularly works away from the employer's place of business while making sales and obtaining orders for which consideration is paid on a commission basis is regarded as a commissioned salesman and is not subject to the minimum or overtime wage benefits of the FLSA.

(5) **Computer Employees.** Individuals who are employed as computer systems analysts, computer programmers, software engineers, or other similarly skilled workers in the computer field are not subject to the minimum or overtime wage benefits of the Act.

For many years, most employees of a funeral home, with the exception of managers and high-level administrators, did not qualify for the white collar exemptions. Although funeral directors and embalmers are required to undergo substantial specialized education and training in most states, prior to 2004 the Department of Labor steadfastly maintained that licensed funeral directors and embalmers did not quality as "professionals".

Despite the Department of Labor's position, at least one federal court adopted an opposing view. In *Rutlin v. Prime Succession, Inc.*, 220 F.3d 737 (6th Cir. 2000), the U.S. Sixth Circuit Court of Appeals ruled that a Michigan funeral director who arranged and supervised funerals qualified as a professional. The decision, which is controlling in the States of Michigan, Ohio, Tennessee and Kentucky, found that Michigan's requirements of an associate's degree, one year of mortuary school and the passage of the national board exam and Michigan's licensing test were sufficient to render a funeral director a professional under the wage and hour laws. While the *Rutlin* decision is only controlling in the four states listed above, it helped to encourage the Department of Labor to update its regulations in 2004.

11.4 2004 Update to DOL Regulations

The Department of Labor updated the regulations governing white collar exemptions in 2004. In a significant development, the Department of Labor recognized for the first time that a funeral director and/or embalmer could qualify as a "professional" under the white collar exemptions. However, in order to qualify as a professional under the new regulations, the funeral director or embalmer had to be licensed and work in a state that requires four years of post-secondary education in order to be licensed as a funeral director or embalmer.

Since only the states of Minnesota and Ohio currently require four years of post-secondary education, the new regulations from the Department of Labor had a very limited impact on funeral service. Funeral homes in the states of Minnesota and Ohio could compensate funeral directors and embalmers as professionals and pay them salaries versus hourly wages. However, in all other states, a funeral home would risk Department of Labor scrutiny if it treated a funeral director or embalmer as an exempt professional under the wage and hour laws.

Although the Department of Labor regulations have not been challenged, a 2011 court case raised the issue of whether they established the sole method for a funeral director to qualify as a professional. In *Rowe v. Olthof Funeral Home*, 2011 U.S. Dist. LEXIS 118182 (W.D.N.Y October 12, 2011), a federal trial court for the western district of New York held that a funeral director qualified as a professional even though New York's funeral licensing law required only two years of post-secondary education. The court held that the regulations issued by the Department of Labor, which required four years of post-secondary education, were not the "exclusive" method by which a funeral director could qualify as a professional. Looking at the standards that define a professional, the court held that the plaintiff in Rowe was required as an embalmer to perform work that required advance knowledge in a field of science that is customarily acquired by prolonged course of specialized intellectual study. As such, the court held the funeral director/embalmer to be an exempt professional under the wage and hour laws.

Whether other courts will uphold the decision in *Rowe v. Olthof Funeral Home* is still an open question. However, the *Rowe* decision raises the issue of whether funeral directors in states other than Minnesota and Ohio qualify as professionals under the wage and hours laws.

11.5 Independent Contractors

Many funeral homes utilize individuals to perform specialized services on an irregular basis. For example, the home may use pallbearers, trade embalmers, bookkeepers, and limousine drivers. An issue which often arises is whether these individuals are employees or independent contractors.

Generally, the Wage and Hour Division will consider such individuals to be employees in circumstances where the funeral home dictates the specific details of the individual's job performance. On the other hand, if the factual circumstances indicate that the person rendering services is an independent businessman performing those services without direct and close supervision of the funeral home, an independent contractor status can be supported.

In this regard, the Wage and Hour Division will look at the following four factors:

(1) Is the individual free to perform the services on the employer's premises or elsewhere?

(2) Is the individual in business and performing the same services for other companies?

(3) Is the individual free to set his or her own hours of work? and

(4) Does the individual provide his own equipment or tools?

In determining independent contractor status, all of the factors above are examined and balanced. Applying these factors to scenarios which may occur in a funeral home setting, it is safe to say that an independent hairdresser would probably qualify as an independent contractor. A pallbearer, on the other hand, would probably be regarded as a part-time employee. The determination of a trade embalmer would be a close question that would turn on the particular facts. Obviously, if the funeral home transports the body to the embalmer's place of business, there is an independent contractor relationship. However, if the embalmer is using the funeral home facilities and equipment, and he has no such equipment available, he will probably be regarded as an employee.

11.6 Recordkeeping

With regard to employees that are subject to minimum wage and overtime requirements, the following records must be maintained:

(1) Personal information such as name, address, and social security number.

(2) Hours and day when the work week begins.

(3) The total hours worked each day and each work week.

(4) The total daily and weekly straight time earnings.

(5) The regular hourly rate for any work week when overtime is worked.

(6) The total overtime pay for each work week.

(7) Any deductions from or additions to wages.

(8) The total wages paid each pay period.

(9) The date of payment and the pay period covered.

Records should be maintained for a three year period except for payroll records which are required to be retained for six years in compliance with the requirements of the Internal Revenue Code. The records do not have to be maintained in any particular form and it is not necessary to have a time clock.

11.7 Minimum Wage

As of 2011, the minimum wage rate is $7.15 per hour. However, in several states the minimum wage standards set by state law are higher than the Federal standards. When both State and Federal laws apply, the law setting the higher wage must be observed.

There are provisions under the FLSA that allow an employer to pay apprentices and disabled individuals a wage scale that is lower than minimum wage. However, in order to qualify for this special wage scale, an employer must apply and receive certification from the Wage and Hour Division.

11.8 Overtime Pay

a. General Requirements

Regarding the overtime provisions of the FLSA, all full-time employees that are not covered by white collar exemptions must be paid at not less than 1-1/2 times their regular rate of pay for all hours worked over 40 hours in a workweek. The FLSA does not require an employee to be paid every week. The employer may make wage and salary payments at other regular intervals such as every two weeks, every half month, or every month.

What the FLSA does require is that the minimum wage and any overtime pay required must be computed on a basis of hours worked each workweek standing alone. An employer cannot average the hours of work over two or more weeks. For example, an employer cannot decline to pay overtime to an employee who worked 50 hours for the first week of the pay period, but only 30 hours during the second week.

How is a workweek computed? A workweek is a regular recurring period of 168 hours in the form of 7 consecutive 24 periods. It need not be the same as the calendar week. It can start on any day at any hour. Once established, however, it cannot be changed unless the change is intended to be permanent.

In determining an employee's regular rate of pay, the following issues may arise:

(1) **Meals and Lodging.** When meals and lodging are customarily provided for the benefit of the employee, the reasonable cost or fair market value of the benefits are considered wages. However, if the facilities furnished by the employer are primarily for the employer's benefit instead of the worker's, their costs may not be considered as wages. The costs of furnishing sleeping quarters to employees who have no other home may generally be regarded as wages under the FLSA.

(2) **Bonuses.** Production bonuses, attendance bonuses and commissions are included in wages. Gifts and discretionary bonuses are generally not included as wages.

(3) **Expenses.** Reimbursement for expenses incurred on the employer's benefit are not included in wages.

(4) **Profit Sharing.** Profit sharing, welfare and thrift plan payments are not part of wages.

(5) **Vacation Pay.** Vacation, holiday and sick pay are not included as wages. Also, premiums paid for holiday, Saturday and Sunday work which is over the time and one-half pay scale are also not included in wages.

b. Salaried Employees

Although an employee may be hired as a salaried worker, the employee is regarded for wage and hour purposes as an hourly employee unless he or she is covered by one of the white collar exemptions. For example, if a funeral home hires an employee for $30,000 per year, for wage and hour purposes, the employee is being paid $600 per week or $15.00 per hour. For any workweek where the individual works in excess of 40 hours, he or she must be compensated time and one-half, or $22.50, for each hour over 40 hours.

c. Variable Workweek Arrangement

One alternative to the regular overtime requirements is the Variable Workweek Arrangement. This is also known as a Fluctuating Workweek Arrangement. The primary advantage to the Variable Workweek Arrangement is that it permits an employer to pay half time for overtime rather than time and a half.

A Variable Workweek Arrangement guarantees the employee a base weekly salary regardless of the number of hours worked. For example, if an employee has a $500 guaranteed weekly salary, he or she must be paid $500 a week regardless of whether the individual works less than 40 hours.

If an employee under a Variable Workweek Arrangement works in excess of 40 hours, the employee is entitled to one-half of the regular hourly rate as overtime compensation. The difficulty in administering a Variable Workweek Arrangement is determining the employee's regular hourly rate. The regular hourly rate will fluctuate depending upon the number of hours that the employee works. To determine an employee's hourly rate, one must divide the guaranteed salary by the number of hours worked during the particular workweek.

For example, if an employee is guaranteed $1,000 a week and he works 50 hours in particular workweek, the hourly rate for that workweek is $20.00. As compensation for that workweek, the employee would receive the regular $1,000 guaranteed salary. In addition, the employee would receive one-half of the regular hourly rate for that week as overtime compensation. In this case, the overtime compensation would be $10 per hour or $100 for the total of 10 hours overtime compensation. Thus, gross pay for the week would $1,100.

In a clarification issued by the Department of Labor in 2011, the Department ruled that the payment to an employee of any type of performance bonus or premium would disqualify the employee from being part of a Variable Workweek Arrangement. Therefore, the Variable Workweek Arrangement may not be used if the funeral home intends to pay any type of performance bonus or premium compensation above the regular hourly wage to the employee .

11.9 Equal Pay Act

Under the Equal Pay Act, employers may not discriminate on the basis of sex by paying employees of one sex at rates lower than they pay employees of the opposite sex in the same establishment, for doing equal work on jobs requiring substantially equal skill, effort and responsibility, and which are performed under similar working conditions. The Equal Pay Act covers executive, administrative and professional employees who, as detailed above, are exempt from the minimum wage and overtime coverage of the FLSA.

The Equal Pay Act permits unequal pay if it can be shown that the wage differential is based on a seniority system, a merit system or on any other factor other than sex. Employers should know that violations of the Act are subject to back pay claims in the same manner as minimum wage and overtime pay violations of the FLSA.

11.10 Particular Wage and Hour Issues for Funeral Homes

a. Caretaker

Oftentimes, a funeral home will have an elderly caretaker who lives at the funeral home. The caretaker may perform very light duties or no duties at all. His or her primary purpose is to provide security for the funeral home and perhaps to answer the phones during off-hours.

The problem presented by the caretaker is whether the caretaker is an hourly employee that must be compensated for each hour the caretaker is at the funeral home. The Department of Labor has attempted to address issues such as this one with the following regulation:

> "An employee who resides on his employer's premises on a permanent basis for an extended period of time is not considered as working all the time he is on the premises. Ordinarily, he may engage in normal private pursuits and thus have enough time for eating, sleeping and entertaining and other periods of complete freedom from all duties when he may leave the premises for the purposes of his own. It is of course difficult to determine the exact hours worked under these circumstances and any reasonable agreement of the parties which takes into consideration all of the pertinent facts will be accepted."

As the above regulation shows, an individual is not deemed to be working simply because the person is on the premises. Presumably, the elderly caretaker would only be working during the time that he or she was performing light duties or answering the telephone for the funeral home. Technically, the caretaker should thus be paid at least the minimum wage for the time responding to telephone calls and performing light duties. However, funeral homes may offset those wages in exchange for the free lodging which is provided the caretaker.

To protect the funeral home, it is recommended that the caretaker of the funeral home enter into a simple agreement by which the caretaker agrees to answer the phone and perform other specified light duties in exchange for free lodging. An alternative to this would be to pay the caretaker minimum wage for his or her actual working time.

b. On Call Employees

Funeral homes often require their employees to be on-call so that they may respond to death calls. An issue which often arises is whether the on-call employee must be compensated for the time on call but away from the funeral home premises.

Generally, employees who are required to be on-call will not be considered to be working if the arrangement with the employer is considered to be one in which the employee is "waiting to be engaged." On the other hand, the employee will be considered to be working for the entire period if it is determined that he or she is "engaged to wait."

The determination of whether an employee is "waiting to be engaged" or "engaged to wait" turns on the freedom of the employee to engage in a personal activities. To the extent that the arrangement substantially restricts any movement by the employee, there is an issue as to whether or not the employee is working during the waiting period.

If, for example, an employee was required to man the telephone at the funeral home and could not leave the funeral home premises, the employee would be regarded as being "engaged to wait." If, however, the telephone could be put on call forwarding to the employee's home or cell phone and the employee could engage in personal pursuits, the employee would be waiting to be engaged and would not be on the clock.

The best solution to the on-call issue is to provide cell phones, beepers, or two-way messaging to on-call employees so that their freedom of movement is not restricted. Assuming they are not on-call an inordinate amount of time, the funeral home will be able to withstand any subsequent challenges by the Wage and Hour Division.

Chapter Twelve

FEDERAL EMPLOYMENT LAW

12.1 Introduction

In addition to the Wage and Hour laws, two other federal statutes place substantial regulatory responsibilities on the funeral director in his or her role as employer. Correspondingly, these statutes provide significant protections to funeral directors and others who are funeral home employees or applicants for employment. Therefore, whether the funeral director is in the role of employer or employee, these statutes can have a direct impact on his or her employment relationships.

12.2 Americans with Disabilities Act

a. Overview

In Chapter Nine there was an examination of how the Americans with Disabilities Act ("ADA") requires funeral homes as public accommodations to make their facilities accessible to disabled members of the public. The ADA also impacts funeral homes as employers by imposing detailed regulations on the treatment of employees and applicants for employment who have disabilities.

b. Coverage of ADA

Funeral homes that employ 15 or more employees fall under the coverage of the employment-related provisions of the ADA. Funeral homes with less than 15 employees are exempt from the ADA's employment-related provisions.

With funeral homes often employing part-time and casual labor, how does a funeral home determine the number of employees it has? Generally, if a funeral home employs 15 or more employees for each working day in each of 20 or more calendar weeks in the current or the preceding calendar year, it will be covered by the employment provisions of the ADA. Therefore, funeral directors may have to make a detailed examination of past employment records to determine if they are covered by this section of the ADA. In making the determination, it is necessary to include all employees, part-time and casual, in the calculation.

c. Purpose of the ADA

Generally, the purpose of the employment provisions of the ADA is to prohibit employers from discriminating against disabled individuals in all phases of the employment relationship — job application and testing procedures, hiring, advancement, discharge, compensation, and job training. This does not mean that an employee with a disability is to be given preference over one without disabilities. The ADA does not establish quotas or preferences. It merely prohibits the employer from considering the fact that an individual is disabled in making certain employment decisions.

In a nutshell, the ADA protects "qualified individuals with a disability." In order to be a qualified individual with a disability, the employee must be able to perform the "essential functions" of the job with or without "reasonable accommodations." Employers are required by the ADA to supply reasonable accommodations on the job to a disabled individual unless to do so would constitute an "undue hardship."

As evident from the above summary of the ADA's employment-related provisions, whether the ADA applies in many employment decisions will turn upon how subjective terms such as "disability", "essential functions", "reasonable accommodations", and "undue hardship" are defined. While the regulations issued by the Equal Employment Opportunity Commission ("EEOC") to interpret this part of the ADA give some guidance, in many situations the precise scope of these terms must be decided on a case-by-case basis.

d. Disability

A "disability" is any physical or mental impairment that substantially limits one or more life activities, a record of having such an impairment, or being regarded as having such an impairment. Mental and physical impairments can include mental retardation; organic brain syndrome; emotional or mental illness; special learning disabilities; orthopaedic, visual, speech and hearing impairment; cerebral palsy; epilepsy; muscular dystrophy; multiple sclerosis; HIV infection; cancer; heart disease; diabetes; cosmetic disfigurement; anatomical loss; drug addiction; and alcoholism.

Although drug addiction and alcoholism are disabilities, individuals currently taking illegal drugs or alcohol are not protected by the ADA. Also, the definition of disability does not include homosexuality or bisexuality; transvestism, exhibitionism, gender identity disorders, or other sexual behavior disorders; compulsive gambling; kleptomania; or pyromania.

There are two steps involved in determining whether an individual is a "qualified individual with a disability." First, this determination concerns whether the individual has the prerequisites for the position to be filled, such as appropriate educational background, employment experience, skills, or licenses. The second determination to be made is whether or not the individual can perform the essential functions of the position with or without reasonable accommodation.

These two determinations must be made at the time the employer is making the employment decision. The employer cannot base the decision on speculation regarding the employee's future inability to perform the job, the risk the employee may become disabled in the future, or the potential increase in health insurance cost which may result from the employee's disability.

e. Americans With Disability Act Amendment Act

In 2008, Congress enacted the Americans With Disabilities Act Amendment Act ("ADAAA") to roll back restrictions that the Supreme Court had placed on the definition of a "disability." While the ADAAA retained the definition of disability as a physical or mental impairment that substantially limits a major life activity, the law made a number of changes. First, it expanded the category of major life activities to include basic activities such as eating, bending, concentrating, thinking, and communicating. It also added major bodily functions such as cell growth, digestion, and neurological, respiratory and circulatory functions. The ADAAA also restricted employers from considering the use of mitigating factors when determining whether an impairment is a disability. For example, simply because an employee can overcome an impairment with medical equipment such as hearing aids, prosthesis, mobility devices, or medications, that does not eliminate that impairment from being regarded as a disability.

f. Essential Functions

In order to determine if an individual can perform the essential functions of a job, it is imperative to first know what those functions are. Understandably, the EEOC did not attempt to define those functions for each of the hundreds of occupations that exist today. Rather, the EEOC has indicated that it will look in the first instance to the employer's judgment as to what functions of a particular job are essential. However, in order for the employer's list of essential functions to be considered as evidence, the list must be prepared in written form PRIOR to the advertising of the job opening or the interviewing of job applicants.

In drafting the list of the essential functions of a job, what factors should be considered by the employer? Generally, essential functions are job duties that are fundamental and not marginal. Factors to be considered are:

- The importance of the function to the overall job.
- Whether there are other employees who can perform the function in question.
- Whether the function is so highly specialized that the employee must perform it because of his particular expertise or ability.
- What is the relative amount of time that an employee holding the position would spend performing the particular function?
- What are the consequences of having other employees perform the function or of not having the function performed at all?
- Do current holders of the job perform the function and, if so, how much time do they spend performing that function?

In interviewing all job applicants, the employer would provide the applicant with the written list of the essential functions of the job and ask the applicant whether he or she can perform each of the essential functions with or without a reasonable accommodation. Generally, it is the responsibility of the job applicant or the disabled employee to inform the employer that an accommodation is needed. Once the employer has learned that an accommodation is needed, the employer and the employee/applicant should meet to determine the following: (1) what are the precise job-related limitations imposed by the applicant/employee's disability and how can these limitations be overcome; (2) what potential accommodations are available and what will be their effectiveness in enabling the individual to perform the essential functions of the job; and (3) what are the individual's accommodation preferences?

It is, of course, impossible to list all possible accommodations which could or may be made. However, examples of the types of accommodations which may have to be made include the following: installing ramps, modifying work areas and restrooms so they are accessible; job restructuring; modified work schedules; reassignment to vacant positions; permitting the use of accrued paid leave or providing additional unpaid leave for necessary treatment; providing reserved parking spaces; and acquiring or modifying equipment or devices such as page turners, lifting devices, telephone handset amplifiers, telecommunication devices for deaf persons, and raised or lowered furniture.

Employers should note that a reasonable accommodation need not be the best accommodation possible, but must sufficiently meet the job-related needs of the individual being accommodated. Furthermore, the employer is generally not required to provide a disabled employee with accommodations that are primarily for the personal benefit of the disabled individual, such as those that assist the individual throughout his daily activities both on and off the job. For example, an employer is generally not required to provide a disabled employee with artificial limbs, wheelchairs or eyeglasses.

g. Undue Hardship

The failure to provide reasonable accommodations may be justified where the employer can demonstrate that the accommodation would impose an undue hardship on the operation of its business. Of course, for an accommodation to constitute an undue hardship it must require more than a "de minimis" expense or inconvenience.

Whether a reasonable accommodation imposes an undue hardship on an employer must be determined on a case-by-case basis. Obviously, what is an undue hardship for a small employer may not be an undue hardship for a large scale employer. The following 11 factors are relevant in determining whether an undue hardship exists:

- The nature and cost of the accommodation required;
- The overall financial resources of the facility involved in the provision of the reasonable accommodation;
- The number of the persons employed at the facility;

- The effect of the reasonable accommodation on expenses and resources;
- The impact of the accommodation on the operation of the facility;
- The overall resources of the employer;
- The overall size of the employer's business with respect to the number of employees;
- The number, type and location of its facilities;
- The type of operation of the employer, including the composition, structure and function of its workforce;
- The geographic separateness of the facility; and
- The administrative or fiscal relationship of the facility to the employer.

The concept of undue hardship takes into account not only financial difficulties but any substantial or disruptive interference caused by the accommodation. For example, if an employee requested the employer to raise the thermostat as an accommodation, such an accommodation may create an undue hardship for other employees, patrons or customers. In such a case, the employer would be justified in refusing the accommodation.

12.3 Civil Rights Laws

a. Overview

Title VII of the Civil Rights Act of 1964, 42 USC § 2000 et seq. (as amended), prohibits discriminatory practices in employment based on race, color, religion, sex, or national origin. Title VII was amended in 1978 by the Pregnancy Discrimination Act which makes it unlawful for an employer to discriminate against a pregnant woman in employment decisions. Another important protection for employees was provided by the Age Discrimination in Employment Act ("ADEA") 29 USC § 621 et seq. (as amended), which prohibits an employer from refusing to hire, discharging, denying employment, or making any employment decision on the basis of an individual's age. The ADEA provides protection only to those who are forty years or older.

b. Coverage of the Civil Rights Laws

The Civil Rights Act, including the Pregnancy Discrimination Act, applies to all employers having 15 or more employees. The coverage of the ADEA is restricted to employers with 20 or more employees. To determine whether part-time or casual labor should be counted, funeral homes should utilize the same test that applies under the employment related sections of the ADA. Therefore, if the funeral home employs 15 or more employees for each working day in each of 20 or more calendar weeks in the current or preceding calendar year, it will be covered by the Civil Rights Act. (The threshold for the ADEA is 20 employees).

Although funeral homes with less than 15 employees are exempt from the Civil Rights Act, it must be pointed out that 45 states have enacted laws which are similar or even go beyond the Civil Rights Act in protecting employees. Also, as a general rule, most of these state laws cover all employers in the state. Therefore, although smaller funeral homes may be exempt from the Civil Rights Act, they are probably subject to similar restrictions under state law.

c. Scope of the Civil Rights Laws

The trio of Civil Rights Laws generally prohibit an employer from basing employment-related decisions on race, color, religion, sex, national origin, pregnancy or age. Prior to 1991, if an employer could show that, although an impermissible factor had entered into an employment decision, the same decision would have been made based on other permissible factors, then no violation of the Civil Rights Act occurred. However, with the amendment of the Civil Rights Act in 1991, if there is any showing that a discriminatory motive entered into the decision, a violation of the Civil Rights Act has taken place.

Because of the 1991 amendments to the law, it is vital for employers to institute safeguards against impermissible motives becoming part of employment-related decisions. This is especially true in hiring employees. It is critical that employers utilize employment applications that have been reviewed for any inquiries into race, religion, age, national origin, sex, and disabilities. Equally important, the representative of the employer conducting the interview of applicants must be trained to avoid any discussions of these prohibited topics.

Decisions regarding promotions, compensation, benefits, discipline, and discharges must also be made without regard to any of the prohibited factors. Employers now routinely utilize employment manuals, periodic written employee evaluations, and detailed employment files to protect themselves against claims under these statutes. Generally, the wisest advice to employers is to thoroughly document all employment related decisions so that there is a written record of why and how the decision was made.

d. Enforcement

Title VII of the Civil Rights Act is enforced by the Equal Employment Opportunity Commission ("EEOC"). The EEOC carries out its mission through a two-step process – mediation and enforcement.

Whenever employees or a job applicants feel that they were victims of discrimination, they must first file a claim with the EEOC or similar state agency before proceeding to court. That charge must generally be filed within six months of the alleged discriminatory practice. The EEOC will alert the employer of the charge and begin a broad investigation. Generally, the investigator will interview the charging party and any witnesses. The investigator will then interview the employer and any witnesses for the employer. An investigation may include an on-site tour with an interview of other employees.

Employers will also generally be requested to produce payroll records, timesheets, seniority lists, job descriptions, employee manuals and handbooks and personnel records.

Within 120 days after the charge is filed with the EEOC, the investigator will make a determination of "cause" or "no cause". If a no cause determination is made, the EEOC charge is dismissed. The complainant then receives a Right-to-Sue letter which allows the complainant 90 days in which to file a private action in federal court.

If the EEOC finds that there is cause to believe a violation of Title VII has occurred, it will attempt to work out a settlement between the complainant and the employer. If this consultation process is not fruitful, the EEOC can file an action in federal district court or can issue a Right-to-Sue letter to the complainant so that a suit can be filed in federal court.

Because of the EEOC's broad investigatory powers, it is important for funeral directors to maintain clean paper trails. The EEOC requires all employers to maintain for at least six months after any personnel action all records related to such action, such as employment application forms, hiring records, demotions, promotions, transfers, layoffs, and termination records, pay rates and training and apprentice selection records. It is generally recommended to employers that all such records be maintained for up to three years.

Chapter Thirteen

OCCUPATIONAL SAFETY AND HEALTH ACT

13.1 Overview

In 1970, Congress enacted the Occupational Safety and Health Act. That Act created the Occupational Safety and Health Administration ("OSHA") within the Department of Labor. OSHA has been charged with the responsibility to protect the nation's employees by implementing new safety and health programs, providing research into occupational safety, instituting a reporting and recordkeeping system to track job related injuries and illness, establishing training programs, and developing and enforcing mandatory job safety and health standards.

In general, OSHA extends to all employers in the 50 states, the District of Columbia and all other territories under federal government jurisdiction. Coverage is provided directly by federal OSHA or through an OSHA-approved state program. Approximately half of the states conduct OSHA-approved state programs. Five of those states, California, Maryland, Minnesota, Tennessee and Washington, have imposed stricter standards than those maintained by OSHA.

Any person or business that is engaged in business and has employees is subject to OSHA. However, OSHA does not cover self-employed persons. Therefore, if a funeral home is a sole proprietorship with the owner serving as the only employee, the funeral home would not be subject to OSHA requirements.

13.2 Enforcement

To enforce its standards, OSHA is authorized under the Act to conduct workplace inspections. OSHA compliance officers will conduct the inspection. Typically, such inspections can be triggered by fatal accidents on the job site, employee complaints, or random inspections of any industry that OSHA is targeting. Following the inspection, the OSHA officer will conduct a closing conference with the employer to discuss all unsafe or unhealthful conditions observed on the inspection. At this time, all apparent violations for which a citation may be issued are discussed. The compliance officer will submit a report to the OSHA area director with a recommendation as to proposed penalties.

The area director may issue citations and propose penalties for those citations. When issued a citation or notice of a proposed penalty, an employer may request an informal meeting with the OSHA's area director to discuss the case. If the employer does not contest the citation, the employer must correct the cited hazard by the prescribed date.

13.3 Notice and Recordkeeping

All employers, including funeral homes, must display OSHA's job safety and health protection workplace poster 2203, or its state equivalent. The poster should be predominately displayed on the bulletin board utilized for employee notices.

As a service industry, funeral homes are exempt from OSHA's basic recordkeeping requirements. These recordkeeping requirements involve the maintenance of OSHA Form 200, which is a basic log and summary of occupational illnesses and injury. OSHA Form 101 is used to supply supplementary information regarding each injury and illness noted on the log. Unless a particular funeral home has been notified by the Bureau of Labor Statistics that it must maintain these records, funeral homes are exempt from these requirements. However, funeral homes in those states with state-approved OSHA plans may have to maintain these basic recordkeeping requirements. In addition, many funeral homes voluntarily maintain these forms.

In the event of an accident at the funeral home involving the death of an employee or the hospitalization of five or more employees, the employer must report the accident to the local or regional OSHA office within 48 hours of the accident. The report must explain the circumstances of the accident, the number of fatalities, if any, and the extent of any injuries.

13.4 General Requirements Standard

As employers, funeral homes are subject to the same general requirements that apply to all other employers subject to OSHA. These requirements are extremely detailed and complex. They regulate items such as the number and placement of fire extinguishers, the posting and lighting of exits, the installation, marking and grounding of electrical equipment and outlets, the width, depth, texture and angle of walking and working surfaces, guards and other protective devices required for the use of machinery and powered lift platforms, and numerous other labels, warnings and signs which must be posted throughout the working environment.

13.5 Specific OSHA Standards Applicable to Funeral Homes

In addition to the general requirements regulations which all employers must comply with, funeral directors are subject to three specific OSHA standards — the Formaldehyde Exposure Standard, the Hazard Communication Standard, and the Bloodborne Pathogen Standard. Each of these standards require affirmative steps and programs which the funeral home must undertake in order to maintain compliance. Although there is some overlap in the requirements of these standards, the funeral director must have a working knowledge of each standard in order to pass an OSHA inspection.

13.6 Formaldehyde Exposure Standard

a. Overview

The Formaldehyde Exposure Standard took effect in 1988. The purpose of this standard is to establish permissible exposure levels for formaldehyde in the workplace. This purpose is accomplished by three basic exposure levels. The first level is the 8-hour Time Weighted Average ("TWA") of .75 parts per million ("ppm"). The second level is the 15-minute Short Term Exposure Level ("STEL") of 2 ppm. Finally, there is the Action Level. If the 8-hour TWA is .5 ppm, the employer has exceeded the Action Level and is required to take certain remedial steps.

Every funeral director with employees is required to conduct formaldehyde monitoring of the preparation room. The 8-hour TWA monitoring should be conducted during peak activities at the preparation room. Of course, the STEL monitoring is to be done during an embalming.

Funeral directors are required to notify employees in writing of the results of the monitoring within 15 days of receiving those results. Retesting should be done whenever changes are made in personnel, equipment or other areas that may cause levels of formaldehyde to increase. All monitoring results should be placed in permanent records.

b. On-going Compliance Responsibilities

If the monitoring reports show that the STEL is below 2 ppm and the TWA is below the Action Level of .5 ppm, the funeral home is not required to take any remedial action. However, the funeral home still has to comply with seven on-going responsibilities under the Formaldehyde Exposure Standard. Those responsibilities are as follows:

(1) **Protective Equipment and Clothing.** Funeral homes must provide protective clothing and equipment to their employees to guard against skin absorption or physical contact with formaldehyde. The equipment must be provided at no cost to the employees. The employer must require that the clothing be worn by any employee that has a potential of coming in contact with formaldehyde.

Protective equipment includes rubber or disposable latex gloves, chemical resistant gowns, goggles, face shields, head and shoe covers, and chemical resistant aprons. Any clothing becoming contaminated must be cleaned or stored with adequate warning so that those who handle it know it is contaminated.

(2) **Hygiene Protection.** Funeral homes must provide change rooms for employees to change from work clothes to protective clothes. In addition, "quick drench" showers must be available in the prep room for any employees who become exposed to formaldehyde. Showers must be in the immediate vicinity of the work area and have the capability to drench the employee quickly and for a continual 15 to 20 minute period. There must also be eye wash

facilities readily available. Eye wash squeeze bottles are not sufficient under the standard.

(3) **Housekeeping.** Funeral homes must institute a visual inspection system of the preparation room to detect any spills or leaks. Of course, all spills and leaks are to be promptly cleaned up by employees wearing protective gear. Formaldehyde waste should be disposed of in sealed containers with warning labels. A written record of inspections and repairs must be maintained.

(4) **Emergencies.** Funeral homes must institute procedures to follow in the event of an emergency due to formaldehyde exposure.

(5) **Hazard Communication.** Funeral homes must assemble Material Safety Data Sheets ("MSDS") on formaldehyde and provide these to the employees. The collection of MSDS is discussed further in Section 13.7.

(6) **Employee Training.** Employees must be trained on the proper use of protective clothing and gear, the cleaning up of spills, the proper handling of formaldehyde, and emergency procedures.

(7) **Recordkeeping.** All applicable records, including the monitoring records, must be maintained for 30 years. Employees should certify that they have received training and a written report of the monitoring results.

c. Remedial Measures

If the monitoring of the preparation room shows that the STEL level is below 2 ppm and the TWA level is below .75 ppm but above the .5 ppm Action Level, the funeral home is required to take the following three remedial steps:

(1) **Formaldehyde Exposure Reduction.** The funeral home shall institute immediate steps to reduce formaldehyde exposure. This can be done by the adoption of safe working practices, the rearrangement of the room so that formaldehyde fumes flow away from the embalmer, and/or the installation of additional ventilation fans. A level of 15 air changes per hour in the prep room is considered to be optimal.

(2) **Periodic Monitoring.** The funeral home must repeat the formaldehyde monitoring at least every six months until the exposure level falls below the Action Level.

(3) **Medical Surveillance.** The funeral home must institute medical surveillance of employees who are exposed to formaldehyde. This requires a medical questionnaire to be answered by the employees under the supervision of a doctor. The questionnaire lists the employee's work history, information about smoking, medical problems, skin problems, etc. If the physician believes there may be an exposure problem based on the questionnaire, he or she is to give a medical exam to the employee. A copy of the physician's written medical opinion is to be provided to the employee and one copy is to be maintained in the employer's records for 30 years.

d. Additional Remedial Steps

If the formaldehyde monitoring shows that the level exceeds the STEL of 2 ppm or the TWA of .75 ppm, the funeral home is required to institute three more additional remedial steps:

(1) **Written Plan.** The funeral home shall prepare a written plan for the immediate reduction of exposure levels.

(2) **Posting of Warnings.** The funeral home shall post warnings on the door of the preparation room alerting anyone who enters about the dangers of formaldehyde.

(3) **Respirators.** If the formaldehyde level cannot be reduced immediately, the funeral home shall provide respirators and institute a respirator program.

13.7 Hazard Communication Standard

The Hazard Communication Standard also took effect in 1988. It is basically a disclosure law so that employees are provided information regarding the hazardous materials they are working with. There are four basic requirements to the Hazard Communication Standard. They are as follows:

(1) **Material Safety Data Sheets.** Funeral homes are required to obtain and maintain Material Safety Data Sheets ("MSDS") from all manufacturers of products used or stored at the funeral home that contain hazardous substances. A Material Safety Data Sheet contains a full disclosure of the product's hazards, precautions in handling the product, and proper steps to take in the event of an emergency.

The funeral home must obtain a Material Safety Data Sheet for each hazardous product. The data sheets, all of which are available on the internet, are to be placed in a three ring binder which is identified as the "MSDS" binder. The sheets are to be arranged in alphabetical order by product name. An index of the products should be prepared and placed in the front of the binder. An MSDS binder should be placed in the preparation room in a designated area with a copy of the MSDS binder in the main office of the funeral home. The MSDS binder may also be in electronic form, but a written backup must be available in the workplace during all work shifts.

(2) **Container Labeling.** All containers of hazardous products must be labeled with the name of the product, appropriate hazard warnings, and the name and address of the manufacturer. Typically, most hazardous products are already labeled by the manufacturer to comply with these requirements.

If the funeral home were to transfer a product from the manufacturer's container into its own container, the funeral home must relabel the new container. The only exception to this requirement is when the product is placed in a container of 10 gallons or less and used immediately.

(3) **Employee Training.** The funeral home must develop a written hazard communication training and information program for its employees. The program shall be provided for all new employees and repeated whenever a

new hazard is introduced into the work area. The program should include information on the labeling of containers containing hazardous substances, the data that is contained on a MSDS, the location of the MSDS binder, the safe handling of hazardous materials, the wearing of protective equipment and clothing, the proper clean-up of hazardous materials, the actions that are to be taken in the event of an emergency, the requirements of the Hazard Communication Standard, and the location and availability of the funeral home's written program for compliance with the Hazard Communication Standard. Employees who have undertaken the training should execute certifications indicating when the training was received.

(4) **Hazard Communication Program.** The funeral home must institute a written Hazard Communication Program which outlines how the funeral home intends to comply with the requirements of the Hazard Communication Standard. The program must be maintained and made available to all employees.

13.8 Bloodborne Pathogen Standard

In 1988, OSHA instituted an interim Bloodborne Pathogen Standard. That standard became final in 1993. The standard contains the following six compliance requirements:

(1) **Exposure Control Plan.** The funeral home must draft a written Exposure Control Plan which explains how the funeral home intends to institute safe work habits and housekeeping practices to minimize exposure to bloodborne pathogens. The plan must include a discussion of the job classifications in which employees have exposure to bloodborne pathogens, how the funeral home intends to implement precautions, training, recordkeeping and hepatitis B vaccine procedures, and the procedure for evaluating exposure incidents.

(2) **Hepatitis B Vaccination.** Funeral homes must make the hepatitis B vaccination series available to employees who have exposure to bloodborne pathogens. The vaccination must be made available at no cost to employees and at a reasonable time and place. Approximately one to two months after the vaccination, HBV antibody testing is required of all employees receiving the vaccination.

(3) **Protective Equipment and Clothing.** As with the other standards, the funeral home is required to maintain and supply protective clothing and equipment for employees that have occupational exposure.

(4) **Training Program.** Each employee with potential occupational exposure must complete a training program when initially hired and annually thereafter. Training sessions must be conducted by individuals with expertise in this area. The training shall include discussions of the Bloodborne Pathogen Standard, a general explanation of bloodborne pathogens and related diseases, the modes of transmission, the use and limitations of personal

protective clothing and equipment, safe work practices, information concerning the hepatitis B immunization program and an explanation of signs and labels. All employees who undergo the training should certify when and under what conditions they receive training.

(5) **Exposure Incidents.** In the event of an exposure to blood or other potentially infectious material, the employer must make available to the exposed employee post-exposure evaluation and follow up.

(6) **Recordkeeping.** Training records must be maintained for 5 years. Medical records for an employee must be maintained for 30 years. Each employee should have a medical records file containing his or her name, social security number, hepatitis B vaccination, record of exposure incidents, and medical evaluations.

13.9 Needlestick Safety and Prevention Act

An important amendment to the Bloodborne Pathogens Standard that impacts funeral service is the Needlestick Safety and Prevention Act which was passed by Congress in November, 2000. This law, which resulted in OSHA's Needlestick Regulation that took effect in April, 2001, requires funeral homes to have a written needlestick exposure control plan that is updated on an annual basis.

In the needlestick exposure control plan, the funeral home must set forth a number of engineering controls to reduce the risk of injury from sharps such as needles, scalpels and syringes. Some of the procedures recommended by the OSHA experts for the National Funeral Directors Association include the following:

- Hypodermic needles should be stored with the covers provided when the needle is purchased. For old stainless steel needles still used by the funeral home, it is not acceptable to store the needles in a piece of cork. Rather, the funeral home should purchase a small piece of tubing to cover the hypodermic needle in its entirety.
- Trocars must be stored with a cover. If a funeral home does not have the cover that was provided when the trocar was purchased, the funeral home can obtain a PCP plastic pipe and cut it so that it is 2 inches longer than the trocar. The trocar can then be placed in the PCP pipe for storage.
- Suture needles may be stored in a large sponge that has been soaked in disinfectant.
- Whenever sharps are removed from or placed into drawers or sterilization containers, the embalmer must use a pair of forceps or a hemostat to retrieve the sharps. Under no circumstances may personnel use their hands.
- Scalpel blades are only to be removed by the use of an engineering control.

Chapter Fourteen

FTC FUNERAL RULE

14.1 Introduction

In 1984, the Federal Trade Commission ("FTC") put into effect the Funeral Industry Practices Trade Regulation Rule (16 C.F.R. Part 453). That regulation, which is commonly referred to as the Funeral Rule, was reviewed and revised in 1994.

The primary purposes of the Funeral Rule are threefold: (1) to give consumers the right to select those funeral goods and services which they wish to purchase; (2) to provide consumers access to detailed, itemized price information prior to purchase decisions; and (3) to prevent misrepresentations and other unfair and deceptive practices in the sale of funeral goods and services.

The Funeral Rule seeks to obtain its objectives by requiring funeral directors to distribute to consumers a series of price lists and documents at various stages of funeral arrangements. These lists must contain itemized prices of the various components of a funeral. Also included in the lists are mandatory printed disclosures informing consumers of the practical and legal necessity of certain funeral goods and services.

Any entity that offers to sell or that does sell funeral goods **and** funeral services is subject to the Funeral Rule. It is important to note that the Rule covers only those that sell both funeral goods and services. Therefore, if a cemetery sells only caskets and vaults, but does not offer funeral services (care of the body, direction of funeral ceremonies), it is not subject to the Rule.

14.2 General Price List

The cornerstone of the Funeral Rule is the General Price List ("GPL"). The GPL is given to the consumer prior to the purchase of the funeral and provides him with a detailed itemized listing of the goods and services offered by the funeral home.

a. Introductory Matters

On the General Price List, the funeral home must place its name, address, telephone number, the words "General Price List" and the effective date of the General Price List.

b. Itemization of Sixteen Goods and Services

To insure that consumers have the right to pick and choose those items which they wish to purchase, the Federal Trade Commission has selected sixteen various funeral goods and services that must be separately priced on the GPL. It is important to note that funeral homes are only required to list these goods and services if they offer them for sale. For example, if a funeral home elects not to offer embalming, it may be deleted from the General Price List.

Funeral homes will typically sell additional goods and services other than the sixteen which must be separately itemized. While funeral homes are not required to place other goods and services on the GPL, as a matter of proper business practice, it is recommended that all goods and services offered by the funeral home be listed on the GPL.

The following is a list of the sixteen goods and services that must be separately itemized on the GPL:

(1) **Basic Services of Funeral Director and Staff.** The basic service fee of the funeral director is the only fee on the General Price List that may be made non-declinable. In other words, the funeral home can require a consumer to pay this charge as a condition of obtaining a funeral. The basic service fee is to include those services that are furnished by a funeral director in arranging nearly any funeral, such as conducting the arrangement conference, planning the funeral, obtaining necessary permits, shelter of remains, and placement of obituary notices. This fee may also include any charges for the recovery of funeral home overhead such as utility expenses, secretarial and administrative costs, insurance costs, equipment and inventory expenses.

(2) **Embalming.** The second price listing on the GPL is the charge for embalming. In addition to the embalming charge, some funeral directors will list additional charges for embalming autopsy cases or tissue donations. This is permissible. (As indicated in Chapter Nine, there cannot be an additional charge for the embalming of contagious diseases cases.)

(3) **Other Preparation of the Body.** Under this category, the funeral home should list any other fees charged in preparing the body. Typical examples include dressing and casketing, hair styling, washing or disinfecting unembalmed remains, and refrigeration charges.

(4) **Services and Facilities for Viewing.** In charging for a visitation, the funeral home should list a fee that covers the services of the funeral director and staff during the visitation as well as the use of facilities. Under this category, funeral homes may have a series of visitation charges. For example, some firms charge according to the length of the visitation (half day, one day, two day) or whether the visitation is pubic or private.

(5) **Services and Facilities for Funeral Ceremony.** As with visitation, the funeral home should list the price of the funeral ceremony. Some funeral homes will list several charges under this category depending upon whether the funeral is conducted at the funeral home or at another location such as a church.

(6) **Services and Facilities for Memorial Service.** A memorial service is a ceremony without the body present. If offered by a funeral home, the funeral home is required to list the price of the service on the General Price List.

(7) **Service and Equipment for Graveside Service.** A graveside funeral service is a ceremony at the graveside when no other funeral ceremony is conducted by the funeral home. This should be distinguished from a committal service which may be included as part of the funeral ceremony. In quoting the price of the graveside funeral service, the charge should include all services and equipment the funeral home will utilize in performing the service.

(8) **Transfer of Remains to Funeral Home.** This charge may be a flat, hourly, or a mileage charge. Many funeral directors impose a flat fee within a certain radius and an excess mileage charge outside of the radius. All charges related to this service, whether it is the use of the hearse or the staff time involved in performing the transfer, must be included in this one charge.

(9) Hearse. Fees for the use of the hearse must be separately itemized. At the option of the funeral home, this charge may be a flat fee, a mileage fee, or an hourly fee.

(10) **Limousine.** As with the hearse, the limousine charge may be a flat, hourly or mileage fee.

(11 **Casket Price Range.** If a funeral home has a separate Casket Price List from its General Price List, it must provide a casket price range of its highest and lowest price casket offerings on the GPL.

(12) **Outer Burial Container Price Range.** As with caskets, if the funeral home maintains a separate Outer Burial Container Price List from its GPL, it must include on the GPL the price range of its highest and lowest price outer burial containers. If the funeral home chooses not to have separate price lists for caskets and outer burial containers, it should list all casket and vault offerings on the General Price List.

(13) **Forwarding of Remains.** The forwarding of remains is one of the four dispositions/funeral services (together with receiving remains, direct cremation and immediate burial) that the Funeral Rule requires funeral homes to present as a package to consumers. In other words, one price should be presented under this listing which will inform the consumer of the total price of forwarding remains. For this reason, a funeral home is required to group all charges relating to this service (service fee, transportation, embalming) into one charge.

(14) **Receiving Remains.** As with forwarding remains, this package offering must present one price to the consumer that covers all components of the receiving of remains from another funeral home.

(15) **Direct Cremations.** A direct cremation is a disposition of human remains by cremation without formal viewing, visitation or any other ceremony with the body present. If a funeral home offers direct cremation, it is obligated to list it as a package on the GPL. In addition, the funeral home is required to offer several package offerings under direct cremation. For example, the funeral home must quote the price of a direct cremation if the consumer elects to utilize his own container and the price of a direct cremation if

the consumer purchases a container from the funeral home. If a funeral home offers direct cremation, it must make alternative containers available to consumers.

(16) **Immediate Burials.** An immediate burial is a disposition of the body by burial, without formal viewing, visitation or ceremony with the body present, except that it may contain a graveside service. The price listing for immediate burials is very similar to direct cremation. The funeral home must provide a range of the lowest and highest priced immediate burial package offerings. It is also required to present various immediate burial package options, including the price of an immediate burial if the purchaser supplies his or her own container.

With the four alternative services of forwarding remains, receiving remains, direct cremation and immediate burial, a funeral home may incorporate into the package price its entire basic service fee or, if it wishes, a proportionate share of its basic service fee.

c. Mandatory Disclosures

There are six separate mandatory disclosures which must appear on the GPL. On the sample GPL that has been placed in the appendix to this chapter, the six mandatory disclosures appear in italicized print so that you can identify them.

Funeral directors are prohibited from editing or modifying the mandatory disclosures. They should appear on the funeral home's General Price List in the exact wording which is provided in the sample model. Also, the mandatory disclosures must be printed in a clear and conspicuous manner. This means that the mandatory disclosure should not appear in smaller type than the other printed materials on the GPL.

The six mandatory disclosures are as follows:

(1) **Choice of Goods and Services.** The first mandatory disclosure on the GPL sample is the disclosure that informs consumers of the right to choose any goods and services they wish. This disclosure should be printed immediately above the itemized price listings of the sixteen goods and services described above.

(2) **Non-Declinable Service Fee.** Under the Basic Services of Funeral Director and Staff on the sample GPL, the second mandatory disclosure is printed. This mandatory disclosure informs consumers that the basic service fee is non-declinable and that it has been included in the charges for direct cremation, immediate burial, and forwarding and receiving of remains. This mandatory disclosure must be made in immediate conjunction with the listing of the Basic Services of Funeral Director and Staff.

(3) **Embalming Disclosure.** In conjunction with the embalming listing, consumers must be informed of their right to decline embalming. The mandatory disclosure which accompanies the embalming price listing on

the GPL sample is designed to accomplish this purpose. This disclosure must be printed in immediate conjunction with the price listing for embalming.

(4) **Availability of Casket Price Lists.** On page 2 of the sample GPL the funeral home has listed its casket price range. Immediately under the casket price range, a mandatory disclosure informs consumers about the availability of a complete price list at the funeral home.

(5) **Availability of Outer Burial Container Price Lists.** As with the casket price range, in immediate conjunction with the outer burial container price range, the funeral home must print the mandatory disclosure which informs consumers that a complete price list of outer burial containers will be provided at the funeral home.

(6) **Alternative Containers for Direct Cremation.** At the bottom of page 3 of the sample GPL there is a listing for direct cremations. Under that listing appears the mandatory disclosure that informs consumers that they can use an alternative container. The disclosure also briefly describes the mandatory disclosure. This disclosure must be made in immediate conjunction with the price range for direct cremation.

d. Package Funerals

Although funeral homes are required to itemize funeral goods and services, they are free to offer package selections. In other words, the funeral home can assemble packages of goods and services and assign one price to it. Additionally, if the funeral home wishes, it may offer these packages at a discount as compared to its itemized pricing. For example, where a traditional funeral selected from the listing of itemized goods and services may cost $6,000, the funeral home could package those goods and services comprising a traditional funeral service and offer it under a package price of $5,500.

If a funeral home chooses to offer a package at a discount, it should not reduce the amount of its basic services fee in arriving at the discounts. Any other items included in the package may be discounted, but not the basic services fee.

While the funeral home is free to offer package pricing, it is important to remember that it must be offered in addition, and not in lieu of, itemized pricing.

e. Distribution of GPL

The GPL must be given for retention to individuals who inquire in person regarding funeral services, specific funeral goods or services, or the prices offered by the funeral home. Whenever there is any face-to-face discussion concerning the overall type of funeral service or disposition, specific funeral goods or funeral services, or the prices for those items, a GPL must be physically handed to the individual making the inquiry. It is not sufficient for the funeral director to simply indicate that a GPL is available if one is wanted.

The GPL distribution requirement is triggered wherever the face-to-face

97

inquiry is made. Therefore, if a funeral director is removing a body from a residence, nursing home or hospital and the family inquires about funeral arrangements, a GPL must be distributed to them. Similarly, since the Funeral Rule applies to preneed arrangements as well as at-need arrangements, the distribution of the GPL should be made to all preneed consumers.

The GPL is to be given to individuals for their retention. Therefore, it is a violation of the Rule to charge a consumer for a copy of the GPL or to require the consumer to return the GPL to the funeral director. It is also improper to place the GPL in a binder or notebook which would implicitly suggest to the consumer that the GPL is not to be retained.

14.3 Casket Price List

If the GPL does not list the retail prices of the caskets offered by the funeral home, a separate Casket Price List must be prepared. This price list is far less complicated than the GPL. Although there are certain items which must appear on the list, there are no mandatory disclosures required on the casket price list.

a. Introductory Matters

On the Casket Price List, the funeral home must place the name of the funeral home, the words "Casket Price List", and the effective date of the Casket Price List.

b. Casket and Alternative Container Listings

All caskets and alternative containers which a funeral home routinely offers for sale must be listed on the Casket Price List, together with the retail price of each. Caskets which require special ordering need not appear on the price list. There are no requirements regarding in what order the caskets and containers must be listed nor are there any requirements concerning what type of caskets must be stocked. However, if the funeral home offers direct cremation, it is required to make an alternative container or an unfinished wood box readily available.

In listing the caskets and alternative containers, the funeral home should provide a brief description of the exterior construction and the interior lining. With metal caskets, the funeral home should list the gauge of the metal. If there is prominent exterior trimming or coloring, this should be noted on the Casket Price List. There is no requirement that the manufacturer, model name, or model number be identified.

c. Distribution of Casket Price List

The Casket Price List must be presented to consumers upon the commencement of a face-to-face discussion about offerings on the Casket Price List or the price of those offerings. The Funeral Rule makes clear that the list should, at a minimum, be distributed to the consumer prior to the funeral director showing casket models to the consumer.

Unlike the General Price List, the Casket Price List does not have to be offered to consumers for their retention. A funeral director may request that the list be returned after the caskets have been shown.

The Funeral Rule allows the Casket Price List to be prepared in alternative formats such as binders, notebooks, brochures and charts. In addition, the FTC Staff has issued an Opinion that allows funeral homes to use software programs that present pictures of caskets in lieu of a written Casket Price List, but only if the computer program shown to the consumer contains all of the required information which must be on a written Casket Price List.

14.4 Outer Burial Container Price List

The requirements of the Outer Burial Container Price List are very similar to those of the Casket Price List. They are as follows:

a. *Introductory Matters*

The name of the funeral home, the words "Outer Burial Container Price List" and the effective date of the Outer Burial Container Price List must be printed at the top of the price list.

b. *Outer Burial Container Listings*

All containers which the funeral home regularly offers should be listed on the Outer Burial Container Price List. Containers that need to be specially ordered are not required to appear on the list. If a funeral home does not offer outer burial containers to its customers, there is no requirement that it prepare an Outer Burial Container Price List.

A brief description of the exterior of the outer burial container should be provided on the price list. Manufacturers, model names, and model numbers need not be listed. In addition, the containers may be listed in any particular order which the funeral home prefers.

c. *Mandatory Disclosure*

As can be seen from the italicized language on the sample Outer Burial Container Price List which appears in the appendix, there is a mandatory disclosure which must appear on the Outer Burial Container Price List. That disclosure informs consumers that Outer Burial Containers are not generally required by law, although many cemeteries make them mandatory. That disclosure may be printed anywhere on the Outer Burial Container Price List.

d. *Distribution of Outer Burial Container Price List*

Whenever there is a discussion of outer burial containers, the funeral director should present to the consumer the Outer Burial Container Price List. As with the Casket Price List, the Outer Burial Container Price List should be given to consumers prior to the funeral director showing any displays or models. The Outer Burial Container Price List need not be given for retention. In addition, the funeral home may utilize brochures, notebooks, charts and computer programs in lieu of a printed Outer Burial Container Price List.

14.5 Statement of Funeral Goods and Services Selected

a. Itemized Entries

The purpose of the Statement of Funeral Goods and Services Selected ("Statement") is to provide consumers with an itemized list of their purchases at the conclusion of the funeral arrangement. To accomplish this, the listings on the Statement must reflect the listings on the GPL. In other words, all separate goods and services which the consumer purchases off the GPL must be identified and listed on the Statement. The itemized price of each good and service must also be written on the Statement. It is improper to lump together on the Statement goods and services which are separately itemized on the GPL. For example, it would be improper to group together all of the separate automotive charges under one fee.

If a consumer purchases a package funeral, the funeral director should list the purchase of the package on the Statement together with the package price. In addition, the funeral director should list on the Statement each good and service that is included in that package. While it is not necessary for the funeral director to separately list the price of each good and service in the package, it is necessary that the consumer have a listing of each good and service that comprises the package.

In addition to the goods and services purchased from the funeral home, the Statement should also list any cash advance items which the consumer purchased through the funeral home. If the actual price of the cash advance item is not known, the funeral director should make a reasonable estimate of the cash advance item on the Statement.

b. Mandatory Disclosures

There are two and possibly three mandatory disclosures which funeral homes must make on the Statement of Funeral Goods and Services Selected. Those disclosures are as follows:

(1) **Listing of Legal and Other Requirements.** At the top of the sample Statement in the appendix is the mandatory disclosure which informs consumers that they will only be charged for those items that they selected or that are required. This mandatory disclosure may be printed anywhere on the Statement, although most funeral homes prefer to put it at the top of the Statement.

The companion requirement to this disclosure is the provision of the Rule which mandates that a funeral home lists on the Statement any legal, cemetery or crematory requirements which compel the consumer to purchase a specific good or service. For example, if state law requires embalming or if the cemetery has a regulation which dictates that outer burial containers must be utilized, those requirements should be listed by the funeral director on the Statement. On the second page of the sample Statement in the appendix, there is a space on the Statement for the funeral director to list laws or regulations which compel the purchase of a good or service.

(2) **Embalming Approval.** The second paragraph at the top of the Statement contains the mandatory disclosure which explains to the consumer the requirements for embalming. As with the previous disclosure concerning legal and cemetery requirements, this disclosure may appear anywhere on the Statement. This disclosure also has a companion requirement which mandates that the funeral director list on the Statement the reason why embalming was performed. On the second page of the sample Statement in the appendix, a blank line has been provided for the funeral director to list the reason why the embalming was selected. Typical reasons include family consent, interstate transportation of remains, or public visitation.

(3) **Marked-Up Cash Advances.** If a funeral home adds a surcharge to a cash advance item or if it receives and retains a rebate, commission or other discount from the supplier of that cash advance item that is not passed on to the consumer, the funeral home has marked-up the cash advance. The Funeral Rule requires funeral homes to identify on the Statement those particular cash advance items that have been marked-up. At the bottom of the cash advance listings on the second page of the sample Statement the required mandatory disclosure appears under which the funeral director would identify those cash advance items that have been marked-up.

If the funeral home never marks-up a cash advance item, it does not have to print this disclosure on the Statement. It should also be noted that the funeral home does not have to identify the dollar amount of the mark-up. It merely has to indicate those cash advance items that have been marked-up. This disclosure must be made in immediate conjunction with the listing of the cash advance items.

c. Distribution of Statement

The presentation of the Statement is to be made at the conclusion of the funeral arrangements. It should be completely filled out and show the total price of the funeral. Signatures are not required on the Statement, although they are recommended since the Statement can serve as the funeral contract. If arrangements are made pursuant to a telephone call, the Statement should be promptly mailed or faxed to the consumer.

14.6 Telephone Price Disclosures

Whenever an individual telephones a funeral home and asks about the funeral home's offerings or prices, the funeral home must provide accurate information in response to those inquiries. The funeral home is prohibited by the Funeral Rule from refusing to give price information over the telephone. Moreover, the funeral director cannot insist upon the caller identifying him or herself as a condition to the disclosure of price information over the telephone.

If a funeral director or trained staff member is not available to provide the requested information, a message should be taken and the call should be promptly returned by the funeral director. Similarly, messages taken by answering machines or answering services must be promptly returned.

14.7 Misrepresentations

The Funeral Rule prohibits misrepresentations in the six specific areas listed below. In addition, the Funeral Rule has prescribed several mandatory disclosures (all of which were discussed earlier) which the FTC believes are necessary to prevent consumers from being misled in these areas.

a. Embalming

The Rule prohibits any misrepresentations regarding the legal necessity of embalming. It is furthermore a violation of the Rule if the funeral director fails to inform the consumer that embalming is not required by law, except in special circumstances. By placing the mandatory disclosure regarding embalming on the GPL, the funeral director has complied with his obligation to inform the consumer regarding embalming.

It is also a violation of the Funeral Rule to inform consumers that embalming is required as a practical necessity in the following cases:

(1) When the consumer wishes to have a direct cremation;

(2) When the consumer wishes to have an immediate burial; or

(3) If refrigeration is available **and** there is to be a funeral with no viewing **and** there is to be a closed casket.

b. Caskets for Direct Cremation

The Rule prohibits a funeral director from representing that state or local law requires a casket for direct cremation. In addition, if a funeral home offers direct cremation, it must make available for direct cremation consumers alternative containers or unfinished wood boxes.

c. Outer Burial Containers

It is a violation of the Funeral Rule to misrepresent that outer burial containers are required by law when such is not the case. It is also a violation of the Rule for the funeral home to fail to affirmatively inform consumers that state law does not require outer burial containers. This duty to affirmatively inform consumers is satisfied by the printing of the required mandatory disclosure on the Outer Burial Container Price List.

Misrepresentations regarding cemetery rules and regulations on outer burial containers are also prohibited by the Funeral Rule. As a precaution against such misrepresentations, funeral directors should obtain updated rules and regulations of local cemeteries so that they are knowledgeable concerning outer burial container requirements.

d. Legal and Cemetery Requirements

The Funeral Rule provides a catchall prohibition against any type of misrepresentation concerning legal or cemetery requirements. In addition, funeral directors are required to list and describe on the Statement of Funeral Goods and Service Selected any legal, cemetery or crematory requirements that compel the consumer to purchase the funeral good or service.

e. Preservative and Protective Claims

Funeral directors may not represent to consumers that funeral goods or services will delay natural decomposition or remains for a long or indefinite period. While the Rule does not prohibit funeral directors from explaining that embalming provides a temporary preservation to the body, it does prohibit any claims that embalming (or any other goods or services) will preserve the body for a long or indefinite period of time.

Funeral directors are also prohibited by the Funeral Rule from making misrepresentations regarding the protective features of caskets and vaults. Any claim regarding the ability of caskets and vaults to protect the body from graveside substances should not be made unless they can be substantiated.

f. Cash Advance Items

If a funeral director marks up cash advance items or receives a commission, rebate or discount which is not passed on to the consumer, it is a violation of the Funeral Rule to represent to the consumer that the charge represents the same amount that the funeral home paid for these items. It is furthermore a violation if the consumer is not informed which particular cash advance item has been marked up. As seen earlier, the funeral director is to identify on the Statement those cash advance items which have been marked up.

14.8 Tying Arrangements

A tying arrangement exists where a seller requires a purchase of an unwanted item in order to obtain a desired good or service. For example, if a funeral director only offers funeral services if the consumer agrees to purchase a casket from the funeral home, the seller has tied the provision of funeral services to the required purchase of a casket. This violates the Funeral Rule.

The Funeral Rule prohibits tying arrangements except in the following three circumstances:

a. Non-Declinable Basic Service Fee

As discussed earlier, the fee for the Basic Services of Funeral Director and Staff may be non-declinable by the funeral director. In other words, it is not a violation of the Rule to require consumers to pay this charge as a condition of receiving funeral services. All other fees, however, must be declinable unless one of the exceptions listed below applies.

b. Legal Requirements

To the extent that state or local law requires the purchase of a funeral good or service, the funeral director may tie the purchase of that good or service to the provision of funeral services. For example, if state law requires embalming of contagious disease cases, the funeral director may require embalming of all contagious disease cases as a condition of providing funeral services.

c. Impossible, Impractical or Excessively Burdensome

The Funeral Rule provides that funeral directors are not required to honor a request for a combination of goods and services that would be "impossible, impractical or excessively burdensome" to provide. Although the funeral director will have to make the initial judgment as to what is "impossible, impractical or excessively burdensome," the ultimate judgment would be made by the FTC if a Rule violation is charged.

The practical necessity of embalming is one area which falls under this exception. For example, a funeral director may refuse a family's request for the public viewing of an unembalmed body on the grounds of practical necessity. It may be offensive to members of the public to view an unembalmed body. Embalming in such circumstances is widely recognized as a practical necessity. On the other hand, if the family requests a brief viewing of an unembalmed body just for family members, the funeral director cannot refuse this request.

d. Third Party Merchandise

As a result of the anti-tying provisions of the Funeral Rule, funeral homes must accept and service merchandise that consumers purchase from other vendors, such as Internet casket sellers, casket store retailers and cemeteries. For example, if a family informs the funeral director that they have purchased the casket from an Internet supplier, the funeral director would violate the Funeral Rule if he or she refused to provide the funeral service to the family or if the funeral home discriminated in any way against the family. Moreover, the charging of any type of fee by the funeral home for handling, inspecting or accepting delivery of the third party casket would violate the Funeral Rule.

The best way to characterize a funeral home's obligation with respect to third party merchandise is to describe it as a "passive" obligation. The funeral home must accept third party merchandise, but is under no duty to actively assist consumers in obtaining, storing or shipping third party merchandise. Therefore, a funeral home that is asked to store a casket that a consumer purchased off the Internet is not required to do so. Similarly, if a consumer requests the funeral home to pick up a third party casket at the airport or shipping terminal, it is not obligated to do so by the Funeral Rule. If the funeral home does accommodate the consumer's request for storage or shipping assistance, it is free to charge the consumer for those services.

Another third party merchandise issue that the FTC Staff addressed in a series of Opinion letters in 2010 concerned unloading and unpacking third party caskets that are delivered to a funeral home. According to the FTC Staff, if a funeral home does not help to unload caskets from casket wholesalers that it buys caskets from, it does not have to help unload third party caskets that are delivered to the funeral home. In other words, funeral homes should treat shippers of third party caskets in the same manner that they treat wholesale casket companies that sell and deliver caskets to the funeral home.

From a practical standpoint, this means that a funeral home would not have to use its personnel to unload caskets or transport the caskets into the funeral home. According to FTC Staff opinion letter, a funeral home should provide a church truck if requested according to the FTC. The funeral home can require the third party shipper to unwrap the casket and take away packing material for proper disposal.

While the Funeral Rule does not permit funeral homes to charge handling or delivery fees for third party merchandise, they may offer discounts to encourage consumers to purchase caskets and other merchandise from the funeral home. This is typically done through package discounts. Funeral homes are permitted to offer funeral goods and services in a package and to discount the price of that package. Moreover, if the funeral home wishes, it may restrict the discounted package only to consumers who purchase a casket from the funeral home. Assuming the dollar amount of the discount is reasonable, the FTC will not regard the discounted package as an impermissible tying arrangement since the consumer who does not wish to purchase the casket from the funeral home always has the option of purchasing funeral goods and services from the funeral home on an itemized basis.

14.9 Prior Permission to Embalm

It is a violation of the Funeral Rule to charge for embalming except in the following circumstances:

a. State or Local Law

Whenever state or local law requires embalming, it is not a violation of the Funeral Rule to charge for embalming that was not authorized by the family. However, funeral directors would be required to note on the Statement that embalming was performed because of a legal requirement.

b. Prior Permission to Embalm

A charge for embalming may be made when the family provides express permission to embalm prior to embalming. It is important to note that the permission to embalm must be expressly provided; it cannot be implied. For example, this requirement is not met if the family gives the funeral director permission to "prepare the body" or if the family desires a funeral service that requires embalming. The funeral director must specifically ask the family for permission to embalm and must receive the permission prior to embalming.

If a funeral director embalms the body prior to receiving permission and if none of the other two exceptions (legal requirements or exigent circumstances) exist, the funeral director may not charge for embalming. This is true even if the family later provides the funeral director with permission to embalm. Charging for embalming under these circumstance constitutes a violation of the Rule.

c. Exigent Circumstances

In order to fall under the exigent circumstances exception, all three of the following conditions must be fulfilled:

(1) The funeral director is unable to contact a family member or other authorized person after exercising due diligence; and

(2) The funeral director has no reason to believe that the family does not want embalming; and

(3) After embalming the body, the funeral director informs the family that if they choose a funeral that does not require embalming, no embalming fee will be charged, but that a fee will be charged if they select a funeral that does require embalming. If the family then selects such a funeral requiring embalming, the funeral director may charge for embalming.

14.10 Retention of Price Documents

Funeral directors are required by the Funeral Rule to retain all price lists for a one year period from the date the price lists were last distributed. Therefore, if a funeral home updates its price list on January 1, 2011, it should retain the prior list until January 1, 2012.

A copy of the Statement of Funeral Goods and Services Selected should be retained for a one year period from the date of the arrangement conference. After the one year time period has elapsed, the funeral director is allowed under the Funeral Rule to dispose of outdated price lists and old statements. Funeral directors should note, however, that certain states may require a longer period of document retention then the Funeral Rule.

14.11 Enforcement

The Funeral Rule is enforced by the Federal Trade Commission. The FTC Staff will respond to complaints from consumers or others regarding violation of the Funeral Rule. Current penalties for a Funeral Rule violation provide for a fine of $16,000 per violation.

One of the principal enforcement mechanisms utilized by the FTC is undercover shoppers who go into funeral homes under the guise of planning preneed funeral arrangements. If the undercover shopper does not receive the price lists in a timely manner, the funeral home will be charged with a Funeral Rule violation. Typically, a funeral home will have to "fail" two different undercover shops in order to be charged with a violation.

If the funeral home is charged with a violation, the FTC will offer the funeral home the option of paying fines under the Funeral Rule or joining the Funeral Rule Offenders Program that is run through the National Funeral Directors Association (NFDA). To join the Funeral Rule Offenders Program (FROP) the funeral home typically pays a fine which is significantly less expensive than the Funeral Rule violation. The funeral home is required to participate in a number of educational and compliance sessions run by NFDA for a three year period. Most funeral homes charged with a Funeral Rule violation opt for participation in the FROP program.

APPENDIX

_____ **FUNERAL HOME**
Address
Telephone Number

GENERAL PRICE LIST

Effective Date:_____

The goods and services shown below are those we can provide to our customers. You may choose only the items you desire. However, any funeral arrangements you select will include a charge for our basic services. If legal or other requirements mean you must buy any items you did not specifically ask for, we will explain the reason in writing on the statement we provide describing the funeral goods and services you selected.

Basic Services of Funeral Director and Staff.......................... $ _____
    Our fee for the basic services of funeral director and staff include conducting the arrangement conference, planning the funeral, obtaining necessary permits, and placing obituary notices. *This fee for our basic services will be added to the total cost of the funeral arrangements you select. (This fee is already included in our charges for direct cremations, immediate burials, and forwarding or receiving remains.)*

Embalming .... $ _____
    Except in certain special cases, embalming is not required by law. Embalming may be necessary, however, if you select certain funeral arrangements, such as a funeral with viewing. If you do not want embalming, you usually have the right to choose an arrangement that does not require you to pay for it, such as direct cremation or immediate burial.

Other Preparation of the Body
    A. Washing and disinfecting unembalmed remains.......... $ _____
    B. Hairdresser .... $ _____
    C. Casketing and Dressing .... $ _____

Additional Services and Facilities
    A. Visitation .... $ _____
    B. Funeral Ceremony.. $ _____
    C. Memorial Service .... $ _____
    D. Graveside Funeral Service .... $ _____

Automotive Equipment
    A. Transfer of Remains to Funeral Home .... $ _____

    B. Hearse .... $ _____

    C. Limousine .... $ _____

Caskets .... $ _____ to $ _____
A complete price list will be provided at the funeral home.

Outer Burial Containers .... $ _____ to $ _____
A complete price list will be provided at the funeral home.

Forwarding Remains to Another Funeral Home .... $ _____
    This charge includes removal of remains, basic services of staff, embalming, necessary authorizations and local transportation to airport. This charge does not include any rites or ceremonies.

Receiving the Remains from Another Funeral Home .... $ _____
    This charge includes basic services of staff, pick up of remains, and transportation of remains to the cemetery. This charge does not include any rites or ceremonies.

Immediate Burials .... $ _____
    This charge includes removal of remains, local transportation to the cemetery, and basic services of the staff. This charge does not include any rites or ceremonies.

    A. Immediate burial with casket provided by purchaser ,,,, $ _____

    B. Immediate burial with casket selected from
        our funeral home (in addition to cost of casket),,,,,,,,,,, $ _____

Direct Cremations .... $ _____ to $ _____
    This charge includes removal of remains, local transportation to crematory, and basic services of staff. This charge does not include any rites or ceremonies. *If you want to arrange a direct cremation, you can use an alternative container. Alternative containers encase the body and can be made of materials like fiberboard or composition materials (with or without an outside covering). The containers we provide are (specify containers).*

    A. Direct cremation with container provided
        by purchaser .... $ _____

    B. Direct cremation with alternative container .... $ _____

_____ FUNERAL HOME

CASKET PRICE LIST

These prices are effective as of _____, but are subject to change without notice.

1. 20 ga. Steel, Sealer Type, Velvet Interior .... $ _____
2. 18 ga. Steel, Bronze Tone, Sealer Type Crepe Interior .... $ _____
3. Solid Bronze, Plated, Sealer Type Velvet Interior .... $ _____
4. Solid Copper, Sealer Type, Crepe Interior .... $ _____
5. Solid Bronze, Scratch finish, Sealer Type, Velvet Interior $ _____
6. 20 ga. Steel, Non Sealer Type, Twill Interior .... $ _____
7. 20 ga. Steel, Light Grey, Sealer Type, Twill Interior .... $ _____
8. Solid Poplar, Velvet Interior .... $ _____
9. Solid Maple, Crepe Interior .... $ _____
10. Solid Oak, Velvet Interior... $ _____
11. Solid Cherry Wood, Velvet Interior .... $ _____
12. Solid Pine, Crepe Interior .... $ _____
13. Soft Wood, Cloth Covered, Twill Interior .... $ _____
14. Heavy Cardboard, Wood Bottom (Cremation) .... $ _____

DISCLAIMER OF WARRANTIES

THE FUNERAL HOME MAKES NO REPRESENTATIONS OR WAR-RANTIES REGARDING THE CASKETS LISTED ABOVE. THE ONLY WAR-RANTIES, EXPRESSED OR IMPLIED, GRANTED IN CONNECTION WITH CASKETS SOLD ARE THE EXPRESS WRITTEN WARRANTIES, IF ANY, EXTENDED BY THE MANUFACTURERS THEREOF. THE FUNERAL HOME HEREBY EXPRESSLY DISCLAIMS ALL WARRANTIES, EXPRESSED OR IMPLIED, RELATING TO THE CASKETS, INCLUDING, BUT NOT LIMITED TO THE IMPLIED WARRANTIES OF MERCHANTABILITY AND FITNESS FOR A PARTICULAR PURPOSE.

_____ **FUNERAL HOME**

OUTER BURIAL CONTAINER PRICE LIST

These prices are effective as of _____, but are subject to change without notice.

In most areas of the country, state or local law does not require that you buy a container to surround the casket in the grave. However, many cemeteries require that you have such a container so that the grave will not sink in. Either a grave liner or a burial vault will satisfy these requirements.

Concrete Box .... $ _____

Concrete with Asphalt Finish .... $ _____

Concrete Strentex Liner .... $ _____

Concrete Marbelon Liner .... $ _____

Concrete Stainless Steel Liner over Strentex Liner .... $ _____

Stainless Steel .... $ _____

DISCLAIMER OF WARRANTIES

THE FUNERAL HOME MAKES NO REPRESENTATIONS OR WARRANTIES REGARDING THE OUTER BURIAL CONTAINERS LISTED ABOVE. THE ONLY WARRANTIES, EXPRESSED OR IMPLIED, GRANTED IN CONNECTION WITH THE OUTER BURIAL CONTAINERS ARE THE EXPRESS WRITTEN WARRANTIES, IF ANY EXTENDED BY THE MANUFACTURERS THEREOF. THE FUNERAL HOME HEREBY EXPRESSLY DISCLAIMS ALL WARRANTIES, EXPRESSED OR IMPLIED, RELATING TO THE OUTER BURIAL CONTAINERS, INCLUDING, BUT NOT LIMITED TO, THE IMPLIED WARRANTIES OF MERCHANTABILITY AND FITNESS FOR A PARTICULAR PURPOSE.

_____ _____ **FUNERAL HOME**

STATEMENT OF FUNERAL GOODS
AND SERVICES SELECTED

Charges are only for those items that you selected or that are required. If we are required by law or by a cemetery or crematory to use any items, we will explain the reasons in writing below.

If you selected a funeral that may require embalming, such as a funeral with viewing, you may have to pay for embalming. You do not have to pay for embalming you did not approve if you selected arrangements such as a direct cremation or immediate burial. If we charged for embalming, we will explain why below.

Funeral Services for

Date of Death   Date of Funeral Service

A. PROFESSIONAL SERVICE SELECTED
  Basic Services of Funeral
    Director and Staff .... $ _____
    Embalming .... $ _____
  Other Preparation of the Body:
    Casketing and Dressing .... $ _____
    Disinfection of Unembalmed
    Remains .... $ _____
    Other .... $ _____

B. ADDITIONAL SERVICES
  AND FACILITIES FEES
    Visitation .... $ _____
    Funeral Service .... $ _____
    Memorial Service .... $ _____
    Graveside Funeral Service .... $ _____
    Other: _____ $ _____

C. AUTOMOTIVE EQUIPMENT
  (local service 25 miles)
  Transfer of Remains to Funeral
  Home... $ _____
  Funeral Coach............................. $ _____
  Limousine(s) .... $ _____
  Other Automotive Equipment:
    _____ $ _____
    _____ $ _____

D. ALTERNATIVE SERVICES
  Forwarding Remains ....$_____
  Receiving Remains ....$_____
  Direct Cremation ....$_____
  Immediate Burial ....$_____
  TOTAL SERVICE SELECTED......$_____

E. MERCHANDISE SELECTED
  Casket .... $ _____
  Outer Burial Container .... $ _____
  Urn.. $ _____
  Clothing .... $ _____
  Registration Book .... $ _____
  Acknowledgment Cards................ $ _____
  Other: _____ $ _____
    Sales Tax................................... $ _____
  TOTAL MERCHANDISE SELECTED $ _____

****

F. CASH ADVANCES
  Cemetery Charges .... $ _____
  Flowers .... $ _____
  Clergy .... $ _____
  Death Certificates .... $ _____
  Other: _____ $ _____

We charge you for our services in obtaining:
  _____
  _____

TOTAL CASH ADVANCES................. $ _____

TOTAL SERVICES, MERCHANDISE
AND CASH ADVANCES .... $ _____
  Paid at or prior to arrangements,
  or other credits .... $ _____

BALANCE DUE .... $ _____

This is a cash transaction. The undersigned jointly and severally agree to pay _____ FUNERAL HOME the balance due on this account, plus the agreed values of such additional services, materials and cash advance as may be furnished by _____ FUNERAL HOME. Such payment shall be made within _____ days from date of the funeral service. A late penalty of _____% per month (_____% per year) will be assessed on the unpaid balance for materials and services.

Reason for Embalming: _____

Legal, cemetery or crematory requirement which compelled a purchase:
_____.

DISCLAIMER OF WARRANTIES

THE FUNERAL HOME MAKES NO WARRANTIES OR REPRESENTA-TIONS CONCERNING THE PRODUCTS SOLD HEREIN. THE ONLY WARRANTIES, EXPRESSED OR IMPLIED, GRANTED IN CON-NECTION WITH THE PRODUCTS SOLD WITH THIS FUNERAL SERVICE, ARE THE EXPRESSED WRITTEN WARRANTIES, IF ANY EXTENDED BY THE MANUFACTURERS THEREOF. THE FUNERAL HOME HEREBY EXPRESSLY DISCLAIMS ALL WARRANTIES, EXPRESS OR IMPLIED, RELATING TO ALL SUCH PRODUCTS, INCLUDING, BUT NOT LIMITED TO, THE IMPLIED WARRANTIES OF MERCHANTABILITY AND FITNESS FOR A PARTICULAR PURPOSE.

Chapter Fifteen

FEDERAL REGULATION OF FUNERAL
BILLING AND COLLECTION

15.1 Introduction

In addition to the Funeral Rule, funeral homes are also subject to several federal consumer protection and disclosure measures that regulate billing and collection practices. Those provisions — the Truth-In-Lending Act and regulations, the Magnuson-Moss Warranty Act, and the Credit Practices Regulation. — were enacted in the past two decades to remedy perceived abuses by retailers and creditors. Since funeral directors are retailers and sometimes act as creditors, it is vital that they possess a working knowledge of these provisions.

15.2 Truth-In-Lending

The purpose of the federal Truth-In-Lending Act (15 USC §1601 et seq.) and the regulations issued pursuant to that Act (12 CFR § 226 et seq.) is to insure that consumers who are provided credit by banks and businesses are fully apprised of all aspects of the credit arrangements. To this end, the Act requires a number of disclosures to be made by banks or businesses extending credit. Since some funeral homes do extend credit and since there is no exemption for funeral homes from the Truth-In-Lending disclosure requirements, it is important to understand under what circumstances funeral homes must make the Truth-In-Lending disclosures.

a. *Coverage of the Act.*

A funeral home will be required to make Truth-In-Lending disclosures during any particular transaction if it satisfies a two-part test: (1) it qualifies as a creditor under the regulations; AND (2) it extends credit to a consumer.

It is important to note that both of these conditions must be satisfied in order to make the Truth-In-Lending requirements applicable. Thus, if a funeral home extends consumer credit in a particular case, but it does not qualify as a creditor under the regulations, it need not make the required disclosures.

b. *Definition of a Creditor.*

As stated above, in order to be subject to the Act, a funeral home must be defined as a creditor. A creditor is defined under the regulations as a person or business which extends consumer credit more than 25 times in a year. In order to determine if a funeral home is a creditor under the Act, one must examine its transactions in the past and present calendar year. For example, if a funeral home extended credit more than 25 times in 2011, it will be defined as a creditor for all of 2012. If it again extends consumer credit more than 25 times in 2012 it will be a creditor for 2013.

Likewise, if a funeral home extends credit 25 times or less during 2011, it will not be a creditor in 2012. However, as soon as it extends credit for the 26th time in 2012, it will be a creditor for the remainder of 2012 and all of 2013. The only way it will be able to lose the creditor status is to extend credit 25 times or less in 2013.

c. Definition of Consumer Credit.

A funeral home extends "consumer credit" whenever it imposes a finance charge in a transaction with a natural person OR it enters into a written agreement with a natural person that calls for payments by more than four installments.

Note that the arrangement must be with a natural person. If the obligor on the funeral bill is a company, the TruthInLending requirements will not apply. This is also true if the obligor is the fiduciary such as a trustee, guardian, administrator or executor of an estate. Since the law does not regard these persons as "natural persons", a funeral home could extend them credit without being subject to the TruthInLending requirements.

A few examples may clarify exactly when a funeral home will be required to make TruthInLending disclosures.

(1) A funeral home has extended credit 30 times in 2011. In 2012, a funeral director at the funeral home orally agrees to allow a consumer to pay the bill in six installments without interest charges. Although the funeral home is defined as a "creditor" for all of 2012, it is not required to make a disclosure in this particular case because it is not extending credit. If the agreement were written or if interest charges were imposed, the disclosures would have to be made.

(2) A funeral home extends consumer credit only five times in 2011. By September, 2012, it has extended credit 25 times. On the next consumer transaction a funeral director agrees orally to allow a consumer to pay in three installments with a five percent finance charge. In this case the TruthInLending disclosures must be made since the funeral home is extending credit (the finance charge) and it is doing it for the 26th time in one year. The funeral home will now be defined as a creditor for the remainder of 2012 and all of 2013.

(3) A funeral home which has extended consumer credit 35 times in 2011 is called on January 2, 2012 by the decedent's sister who is serving as executrix of the estate. The funeral director orally agrees to allow the estate to pay the bill in installments with a finance charge. In this case the funeral home is a creditor for all of 2012 since it extended consumer credit more than 25 times in the previous year. It also would be regarded as extending consumer credit in this transaction, but for the fact that the obligor on the funeral bill is the estate of the decedent. Therefore, since the funeral home is not

extending consumer credit to a natural person, the TruthInLending disclosures are not applicable.

d.   Definition of a Finance Charge.

As stated above, whenever a finance charge is imposed, a person is deemed to be extending credit. This raises the question as to what constitutes a finance charge. Two particular situations which concern funeral homes are the late charge and the discount for prompt payment.

Under the regulations, late charges imposed against consumers not making payments when due will not be considered to be finance charges. However, in order to distinguish a late charge from a normal finance charge, the funeral home must take certain precautions. The invoice or bill must state that the entire amount of the account is due by a certain date, and if not paid in full, a penalty or late charge will be imposed. The funeral home also must impose the charge against all violators on a consistent basis. Furthermore, if a bill is not paid by a certain date, it should warn the consumer by letter or phone call that the account is overdue and that penalties are being imposed. It is important that the funeral home establish some type of collection procedure and that it apply it against all consumers who fail to make payments when due.

In addition to the measures set out above, the funeral home must avoid referring to the late charge as an interest charge, finance charge, carrying charge, or service charge. It is important that the invoice clearly state that the charge is a late charge or penalty imposed for the failure to pay the entire amount of the bill when due.

Until a recent clarification to the Truth-In-Lending, merchants who offered discounts for prompt payments were subject to Truth-In-Lending disclosures. For example, a funeral home that allows a consumer to pay in 30 days, but that offered a 2% discount for payment at the time of service was looked upon as extending credit. That is no longer the case. Therefore, funeral homes may offer prompt payment discounts without being subject to Truth-In-Lending Regulations.

e.   Preneed Arrangements.

Those funeral homes that enter into preneed payment arrangements must be cognizant of the fact that these arrangements may constitute extensions of consumer credit. If the funeral home imposes a finance charge, or if the customer pays for the funeral services in more than four installments pursuant to a written agreement, the preneed arrangements will be extensions of consumer credit. Therefore, funeral homes that enter into these particular types of preneed arrangements must be aware of the fact that if they are parties to 25 or more of these arrangements in one year, they will have the status of a creditor and will be required to make TruthIn-Lending disclosures.

f.   Advertising.

Advertisements that list credit terms are governed by the TruthInLending

Act. The Act has two basic requirements with regard to advertisements. The first is that the specific credit terms listed in the advertisement, i.e., downpayment, amount that will be financed, annual percentage rate, must be the terms that actually are or will be arranged. Secondly, if the advertisement lists any of the following items: the amount of the downpayment required, the amount of any installment payment, the number of payments, the length of the repayment period or the amount of any finance charge, it must also list each of the following items: the amount of the downpayment, the terms of repayment, and the annual percentage rate, using that term. If the annual percentage rate is a variable rate, that fact must also be noted.

g. Refinancing and Extensions.

If a refinancing occurs, an entire set of new TruthInLending disclosures must be made to the consumer. A refinancing takes place when the original credit obligation is replaced by a new credit obligation. If the original credit obligation is only extended or deferred, however, new TruthInLending disclosures need not be made. Likewise, if the annual percentage rate is decreased, new TruthInLending disclosures are not mandated. Finally, if the terms of the credit obligation are changed as a result of a court proceeding, e.g. bankruptcy, no new disclosures are required.

Even though an extension or deferral does not require the issuance of a new set of disclosures, various minor disclosures must be made if a fee is charged as a result of the extension or referral, and the credit obligation is not one in which the finance charge is determined simply by the application of a percentage rate to the unpaid balance. In that event, the creditor must set out the amount of the fee, the amount deferred or extended, and the date to which payment is deferred or extended.

h. Required Disclosures.

If a funeral home has the status of a creditor, it must make the disclosures listed below whenever it extends consumer credit. These disclosures must appear on a separate form from the funeral contract or bill and they must be made prior to the consummation of the sale.

(1) **Amount Financed.** There are two disclosures required under this item. First, the consumer must be told the "amount financed" which is calculated by taking the cash price, adding any other amounts which are advanced by the funeral home but which are not part of the finance charge, and subtracting the downpayment and any prepaid finance charge. The funeral home, in making this disclosure, must use the term "amount financed" and must explain it as "the amount of credit provided to you or on your behalf."

The second disclosure requires an itemized statement by the funeral home of the amount financed. The itemization, which is required to be listed separately from the rest of the disclosures, must state what amount was distributed directly to the consumer, what amount went to the payment of any prepaid finance charges, what amount was credited to the consumer's account with the funeral home, and what amounts were paid by the funeral home to other persons on the consumer's behalf. In regard to this last disclosure, a funeral home would be required to list all cash advance items, such as newspaper charges, cemetery charges, flower charges, etc. and the name of each person the funeral home paid.

However, in place of providing this itemization, the funeral home may provide a statement informing the consumer that he or she is entitled to a written itemization of the amount financed and a space for the consumer to indicate if one is desired. If the consumer does not elect to have one provided, the funeral home is excused from this requirement.

(2) **Finance Charge.** The funeral home must disclose that amount which it is charging to extend the credit. This must be referred to as the "finance charge" and it must be explained as "the dollar amount the credit will cost you." The finance charge is a total of all credit costs including interest, service charge, carrying charge, loan fee, finder fee or similar charges, timeprice differential and credit reports. The cost of insurance premiums must be included as part of the finance charge, unless they are disclosed separately. The finance charge does not include taxes, license fees, legal fees, registration fees and the like.

Under the TruthInLending regulations, if the amount financed is $1,000.00 or below and the finance charge stated is within $5.00 of the actual finance charge, the stated finance charge will be deemed accurate. For all amounts above $1,000.00, the regulations provide a tolerance of $10.00.

(3) **Annual Percentage Rate.** In making this disclosure, the funeral home must use the term "Annual Percentage Rate" and provide the explanation that this is "the cost of your credit as a yearly rate." If it is possible for this rate to be increased after the sale, the funeral home must disclose the circumstances under which the rate can be increased, how the increase would affect the consumer's payments, whether the increase has any limitations, and an example of the payment terms that would result from the increase.

Under the regulations, the stated annual percentage rate will be considered accurate if it is not more than oneeighth of one percent above or below the actual percentage rate. For irregular transactions, such as those where the payments are not equal, the tolerance is increased to onefourth of one percent. In calculating the rate, creditors are permitted to disregard the fact that months have different numbers of days and the occurrence of leap year.

The easiest method to calculate the annual percentage rate is to obtain a copy of the Federal Reserve Board's Annual Percentage Rate Tables, Volume I. A copy may be obtained through the Federal Reserve System, Washington, D. C. 20551 or from any Federal Reserve Bank.

(4) **Payment Schedule.** The funeral home is required to disclose the payment schedule, including the number, amount and timing of all payments. In the case of a demand obligation where there is no maturity date, the funer-

al home is required to disclose the due dates for interest payments for the first year only. In the event that the payments vary because the finance charges apply to an unpaid principal balance, the funeral home must disclose the largest and smallest payments in the series and explain that the payments may vary.

(5) **Total of Payments.** The funeral home must disclose the sum of payments under the payment schedule. It should do this under the heading "Total of Payments" and must explain that term as meaning "the amount you will have paid when you have made all scheduled payments."

(6) **Total Sale Price.** The total sale price is the sum of the cash price, the finance charge and any amount financed by the funeral home which was not included in the finance charge. The funeral home is required to use the term "Total Sale Price" in making this disclosure and must explain that it is "the total price of your purchase on credit, including your down payment of $_____."

(7) **PrePayment Penalty or Rebate.** The funeral home must state whether there is a penalty for prepaying the obligation. Likewise, if the funeral home provides a rebate for prepayment, it must so state.

(8) **Late Payment.** If a charge will be imposed against the consumer in the event of a late payment, the funeral home must disclose the amount of the penalty.

(9) **Security Interest.** If a security interest is obtained by the funeral home, it must disclose that fact and identify the secured property by type or item.

    i.   Multiple Purchasers.

If two or more persons purchase the funeral, the TruthInLending disclosures need be provided only to the primary obligor. If the two persons are joint and equal obligors, the disclosures may be given to either one of them. The funeral home should always provide the customer with the copy of the TruthInLending disclosures and retain the original form for at least two years.

    j.   Disclosure Example.

A funeral costing $4,000 is paid for by a $1,000 downpayment and an agreement to pay off the remaining $3,000 in 12 equal installments at an interest rate of 15 percent. Assuming the funeral home was a "creditor", it would have to make the disclosures which are listed in Figure 15.A at the end of this Chapter.

A brief analysis will show how the disclosures listed in Figure 15.A were determined. The Amount Financed ($3,000) is the cash price of the funeral ($4,000) minus the downpayment ($1,000). The Finance Charge is $249.36. This was determined by adding up the amount of the payments that will be made ($3,249.36) and subtracting the Amount Financed ($3,000). If any additional fee such as credit reports or loan fees were charged to the borrower, these would have to be added on to the Finance Charge.

The Annual Percentage Rate is 15 percent. The Total of Payments ($3,249.36) is arrived at by simply adding up all the payments. The Total Sales Price ($4,249.36) is ascertained by adding the Total of Payments ($3,249.36) with the downpayment ($1,000.00). The Payment Schedule simply sets out the due dates of the payments. In this case, the amount of each payment was determined by using a comprehensive loan amortization book which is generally available at book stores. Finally, the amount of the late penalty is listed and the fact that no security interest has been taken is noted.

15.3 Magnuson-Moss Warranty Act

The Magnuson-Moss Warranty Act (15 USC § 2301 et seq.) is a federal statute which governs express and implied warranties. As a sellers, funeral homes are providing warranties on the merchandise they sell even though they do not manufacture it. For example, when a funeral home sells a casket, it warrants by implication that the casket is structurally sound to hold the body. If the bottom falls out of the casket, the funeral home has breached those implied warranties.

a. Disclaimer of Warranties.

The law allows sellers of merchandise to disclaim these warranties, but only if the seller does it by using specific language that is presented to consumers in a clear and conspicuous manner. At the conclusion of this chapter is Figure 15.B which is an example of an effective disclaimer of warranties. In order to disclaim warranties on the merchandise sold by funeral homes, it is advisable to place this disclosure in bold face print on the Casket and Outer Burial Container Price Lists as well as the Statement of Funeral Goods and Services Selected. (The District of Columbia and the states of Alabama, Connecticut, Kansas, Maine, Maryland, Massachusetts, Minnesota, Mississippi, New Hampshire, Vermont, Washington, and West Virginia prohibit sellers of consumer goods from disclaiming these implied warranties).

b. Adoption of Manufacturers' Warranties.

Although the funeral home as a seller does not offer its own expressed warranties, many of the casket and vault manufacturers do offer warranties on their products. Funeral homes are generally not liable for warranties made by manufacturers. However, funeral homes may be viewed as adopting those warranties if they make certain written or oral representations. For example, if a funeral director assured a consumer that a casket is water-tight, that funeral home may be viewed as the source of that warranty. Funeral directors should insure that they qualify all their claims by saying that it is the manufacturer which warrants that the casket is water-proof, etc. All representations regarding the casket should be tied to the manufacturers' warranties.

c. Display of Manufacturers' Warranties.

As sellers, funeral homes are obligated by law to make available to consumers copies of the manufacturers' warranties. The FTC has enacted regulations under the Magnuson-Moss Warranty Act which require all sellers of consumer products to make available to prospective buyers, prior to sale, the text of any written manufacturer's warranty (16 CFR § 700 et seq).

Funeral homes can comply with the FTC regulation in one of two ways. First, funeral homes can clearly and conspicuously display the text of the warranty in close conjunction with the product being sold. Secondly, funeral homes can maintain a binder or series of binders which contains each warranty. The binder should be labeled "WARRANTIES", should be properly indexed according to product, should be updated as new products are offered, and should be maintained in a location which provides the buyer with ready access to the binder. Either the binder or a sign advising the consumer of the binder's presence must be displayed in a manner reasonably calculated to draw the buyer's notice.

15.4 FTC Credit Practices Regulation

When a funeral home enters into a retail installment contract with a customer by which it permits the customer to pay for a funeral purchase over time through a note, account, or similar debt instrument, the funeral home must insure that the debt instrument is in compliance with the FTC's Credit Practices Regulation. There are six basic requirements with regard to Consumer Credit Practices under the FTC's regulation. They are as follows:

a. *Cognovit Note or Confession of Judgement.*

It is a violation of the Federal Trade Commission Act for a funeral home, directly or indirectly, to take or receive from a consumer a debt instrument that constitutes or contains a cognovit or a confession of judgement, warrant of attorney, or other waiver of the right to notice and the opportunity to be heard in the event of suit or process thereon.

b. *Executory Waiver.*

Debt instruments utilized by funeral homes in retail installment sales to consumers may not constitute or contain an executory waiver or a limitation of exemption from attachment, execution, or other process on real or personal property held, owned by, or due to the consumer unless the waiver applies solely to property which is subject to the security interest which is executed in connection with the obligation. Since most goods sold by funeral homes cannot be attached in a collection suit, funeral homes' debt instruments should contain no executory waivers or limitation of exemptions from attachments.

c. *Assignment of Wages.*

The FTC Credit Practices Regulations also prohibit a debt instrument used by a retail installment seller in a consumer transaction from constituting or containing an assignment of wages or other earnings unless:

(1) the assignment by its terms is revocable at the will of the debtor, or

(2) the assignment is a payroll deduction plan or pre-authorized payment plan, commencing at the time of the transaction, in which the consumer authorizes a series of wage deductions as a method of making such payment, or

(3) the assignment applies only to wages or other earnings already earned at the time of the assignment.

    d.   *Security Interest in Household Goods.*

No debt instrument between a retail installment seller and a consumer may constitute or contain a non-possessory security interest in household goods other than a purchase money security interest. In other words, a funeral home may not take a security interest in clothing, furniture, applications, radios, televisions, linens, china, crockery, kitchenware, and personal effects (including wedding rings) of the consumer in order to secure the purchase of a funeral. It should be noted that works of art, electronic entertainment equipment (except one television and one radio), antiques (any item over 100 years old), and jewelry (except wedding rings) are not regarded as household goods, and therefore, may be used as security.

    e.   *Co-signor Practices.*

Under the Federal Trade Commission Act, it is a deceptive act or practice for a lender or a retail installment seller to directly or indirectly misrepresent the nature or extent of a cosigner's liability. It is also a violation of the Act for a lender or a retail installment seller, directly or indirectly, to obligate a cosigner unless the cosigner is informed prior to being obligated, of the nature of the cosigner's liability. To prevent these deceptive acts, the following notice should be provided to all cosigners on a separate document:

"NOTICE TO COSIGNER

You are being ask to guarantee this debt. Think carefully before you do. If the borrower doesn't pay the debt, you will have to. Be sure you can afford to pay if you have to, and that you want to accept this responsibility.

You may have to pay up to the full amount of the debt if the borrower does not pay. You may also have to pay late fees or collection costs, which increase this amount.

The creditor can collect this debt from you without first trying to collect from the borrower. The creditor can use the same collection methods against you that can be used against the borrower, such as suing you, garnishing your wages, etc. If this debt is ever in default, that fact may become part of your credit record.

This notice is not the contract that makes you liable for the debt."

f. Late Charges.

It is a violation of the Federal Trade Commission Act for a lender or retail installment seller to levy a late charge on a payment which is otherwise a full payment for the applicable period when the only delinquency is attributable to late fees which were assessed on that installment. In other words, a late fee cannot be charged on a timely installment payment if the only problem with that payment is that it did not include a late charge payment for a previous delinquency.

APPENDIX

FIGURE 15.A

TRUTH IN LENDING

DISCLOSURE OF INFORMATION

Funeral Director's Name and Address

Buyer's Name and Address

AMOUNT FINANCED: $3,000.00. The amount of credit provided to you or on your behalf. You have a right to receive at this time itemization of the Amount Financed.

       _____ I want an itemization Buyer's Initials

       _____ I do not want an itemization.Buyer's Initials

FINANCE CHARGE: $249.36. The dollar amount the credit will cost you.

ANNUAL PERCENTAGE RATE: 15% The cost of your credit as a yearly rate.

TOTAL OF PAYMENTS: $3,249.36. The amount you will have paid when you have made all scheduled payments.

TOTAL SALES PRICE: $4,249.36. The total price of your purchase on credit, including your downpayment of $ 1,000.00.

PAYMENT SCHEDULE:

Number of Payments	Amount of Payments	Due Date of Payments
12	$270.78	First of every month for 12 months

LATE PAYMENT: If the amount due is not fully paid by the due date, a penalty will be charged at the rate of 10% per month on the unpaid balance.

SECURITY INTEREST:

       _____ You are giving a security interest in _____.

       _____ You are not giving a security interest.

BUYER ACKNOWLEDGES RECEIPT OF A COMPLETED COPY OF THIS DISCLOSURE STATEMENT PRIOR TO CONSUMMATION OF THE CREDIT SALE. See Contract documents for any additional information about default and nonpayment.

_____   _____

       Date   Buyer's Signature

FIGURE 15.A

DISCLOSURE OF WARRANTIES

_____ FUNERAL HOME MAKES NO REPRESENTA-
TIONS OR WARRANTIES REGARDING THE MERCHANDISE SOLD WITH
THIS FUNERAL SERVICE. THE ONLY WARRANTIES, EXPRESSED OR
IMPLIED, GRANTED IN CONNECTION WITH MERCHANDISE SOLD WITH
THIS FUNERAL SERVICE ARE THE EXPRESS WRITTEN WARRANTIES, IF
ANY, EXTENDED BY THE MANUFACTURERS THEREOF. NO OTHER
WARRANTIES, EXPRESSED OR IMPLIED, INCLUDING THE IMPLIED
WARRANTIES OF MERCHANTABILITY AND FITNESS FOR A PARTICU-
LAR PURPOSE, ARE EXTENDED BY_____FUNERAL
HOME.

Chapter Sixteen

FEDERAL PRIVACY LAWS

16.1 In General

Over the past two decades, Congress and federal agencies have enacted a number of laws and regulations to combat the ever-growing threats of identity theft, credit scams, and other privacy-invasion schemes that have been spawned by the internet and the computerization of America. For the most part, these privacy laws and regulations impose wide-ranging requirements and restrictions on financial and health care businesses that deal with consumers. Since funeral homes engage in sizable financial transactions with consumers and are involved with hospital and health care services on a routine basis, questions often arise as to whether funeral homes are covered by these federal privacy laws and, if so, what are their obligations.

16.2   Gramm-Leach-Bliley Act

One of the earlier laws tackling privacy issues in the financial sector was the Gramm-Leach-Bliley Act of 1999 (the "GLB Act"). The GLB Act and the regulations developed under it are designed to protect the privacy of consumer information held by financial institutions. There are three primary parts to the GLB Act: the Financial Privacy Rule, the Safeguard Rule, and the Pretexting Provisions.

The Financial Privacy Rule is one that most Americans are familiar with since for the past decade consumers have routinely received privacy notices from banks, stock brokers, insurance companies, and other financial institutions. The purpose of the privacy notice is to inform consumers about the type of information the financial institution collects from consumers and what types of businesses or companies they share that information with. If the financial institution is sharing the information with non-affiliated companies, the consumer has the right to "opt out" from the financial institution's disclosure of personal information.

Under the Safeguard Rule, financial institutions are required to set up and maintain safeguards to protect personal financial information obtained from consumers. The regulation requires the use of computer firewalls and encryption devices to protect consumer information. The Safeguard Rule also dictates procedures that financial institutions should follow to destroy consumer financial information, such as the use of shredders and specially designed trash containers.

The third part of the GLB Act prohibits third parties from obtaining personal information through fraud or trickery. The Pretexting Provisions make it a criminal act to falsely obtain personal information from a financial institution or from consumers.

The GLB Act covers not only traditional financial institutions such as banks, stockbrokers, and insurance companies, but also any business that provides financial products or services to consumers. Those non-traditional financial institutions include mortgage lenders, loan brokers, tax preparers, debt collectors, and financial advisors. However, the GBL Act does not cover funeral homes.

According to the Federal Trade Commission, which enforces the GLB Act against non-traditional financial institutions, a business is not considered to be a "financial institution" under the GLB Act unless it is "significantly engaged in financial activities." While funeral homes obviously engage in financial transactions with consumers, some of which are substantial and ongoing (such as a preneed installment contract), that does not mean that the funeral home is "significantly engaged in financial activities." Rather, the primary business of a funeral home is the provision of funeral services, not financial services. Therefore, funeral homes are not covered by the GLB Act and would not be subject to the requirement to issue privacy notices and safeguard consumer financial information.

There are, of course, situations where funeral homes are acting as agents of financial institutions. For example, when a funeral home sells a preneed insurance policy for an insurance company, it is the agent of that insurance company. However, the obligations of the GLB Act are on the insurance company, not the funeral home as the agent. Therefore, it is the insurance company that would be required to issue privacy notices and safeguard consumer information under the GLB Act, not the funeral home.

16.3 HIPAA

The most significant protection of patients' medical and health information originated with the 1996 passage of the Health Insurance Portability and Accountability Act ("HIPAA"). That Act required the U.S. Department of Health and Human Services ("HHS") to issue regulations protecting the privacy of health information. HHS subsequently developed the Standards for Privacy of Individually Identifiable Health Information, which is now commonly referred to as the HIPAA Privacy Rule.

The businesses covered by the HIPAA Privacy Rule (the "Covered Entities") generally include health care providers, health care billing and payment services, and health plans. The HIPAA Privacy Rule requires Covered Entities to undertake the following actions:

- Notify patients about their privacy rights and how their health information will be used.
- Adopt and implement privacy procedures for the Covered Entity.
- Train employees so that they understand the privacy procedures.

- Designate an individual to be responsible for seeing that privacy procedures are adopted and followed.
- Secure patient records containing individually identifiable health information so that they are not readily available to unauthorized parties.

When a Covered Entity has another business perform functions or activities on behalf of the Covered Entity, and that business is provided patient health information, the business is regarded as a "Business Associate" of the Covered Entity. Until this year, the HIPAA Privacy Rule did not directly regulate Business Associates, but did require Covered Entities to oversee the activities of Business Associates. With amendments passed by Congress in 2009, HHS is now considering direct regulation of Business Associates under the HIPAA Privacy Rule.

The important thing for funeral homes to understand is that they are neither Covered Entities nor Business Associates. As reviewed above, Covered Entities are generally health care providers, health care insurers, and medical billing services. As such, funeral homes are not Covered Entities.

Funeral homes also do not generally contract with Covered Entities to perform functions or activities on behalf of the Covered Entities. Therefore, funeral homes do not qualify as Business Associates. While funeral homes may receive health care information from Covered Entities, such as a hospital disclosing to a funeral home that an individual died of a contagious disease, the funeral home still is not regarded as a Business Associate.

Although funeral homes are not covered by the HIPAA Privacy Rule because they are neither Covered Entities nor Business Associates, the HIPAA Privacy Rule does recognize that there are legitimate needs to disclose individual health information to third parties, such as funeral homes. The HIPAA Privacy Rule does not mandate the disclosure of confidential health information to third parties such as funeral homes. Rather, the HIPAA Privacy Rule allows Covered Entities to make those disclosures either as a voluntary reporting practice or as a reporting practice that may be compelled by state law.

Fortunately for funeral homes, the HIPAA Privacy Rule recognizes that funeral directors may be included in the class of businesses and individuals receiving confidential privacy information. Section 164.512(g) of the Rule allows Covered Entities to disclose confidential health information to funeral directors consistent with applicable law, as necessary to carry out their duties with respect to a decedent. For example, the Rule allows hospitals to disclose to funeral directors the fact that an individual has donated an organ or tissue because this information has implications for funeral home staff when embalming a decedent. The Rule also states that when necessary for funeral directors to carry out their duties, Covered Entities may disclose protected health information prior to and in reasonable anticipation of an individual's death.

Some states require disclosure of patient health information to funeral homes, such as the results of a positive HIV test or the presence of a communicable disease. Other states do not require these disclosures. To determine what disclosures a particular state may or may not require, a funeral home may click on www.healthprivacy.org and refer to its state law. That website has a survey of each state's law regarding disclosure of patient health information.

16.4 FTC/FCC Do-Not-Call Regulation

In 2003, both the Federal Trade Commission and the Federal Communications Commission issued telemarketing sales rules which implemented the national Do-Not-Call List. These regulations allowed consumers to register any residential telephone number, including cell phone numbers, on a national registry at no cost. Companies engaged in telemarketing are subject to a $16,000 fine if they call any number on the Do-Not-Call List. In addition to the Do-Not-Call List, the FTC/FCC telemarketing sales rules also contain a number of restrictions and prohibitions on telephone sales practices.

If a funeral home utilizes telephone solicitation to sell funeral goods or services, or if it allows a third party company or agent to sell on its behalf, it needs to be aware of the requirements of the telemarketing sales rules. The rules not only cover telemarketers, but any company that hires or retains a telemarketer to sell on its behalf. Therefore, a funeral home will be liable if a telemarketer, such as a preneed insurance agency representing the funeral home, violates the telemarketing sales rule.

If a business is involved in telemarketing, it is required to obtain the Do-Not-Call-List and scrub its sales call list against the Do-Not-Call List to ensure that no illegal calls are made. The regulations require that the list be scrubbed every thirty-one (31) days. Telemarketers are able to access the Do-Not-Call List through the FTC website and by area code.

There are several important exemptions to the Do-Not-Call List which funeral homes may take advantage of. First, the Do-Not-Call restrictions do not apply to telephone calls that are initiated by consumers in response to general media advertising or direct mail advertising. Therefore, funeral homes may solicit consumers through general advertising or direct mail advertising and invite them to call the funeral home. Calls made in response to the advertising are not covered by the telemarketing sales rules.

Another important exemption to the telemarketing sales rules are calls made to consumers with which the funeral home has an established business relationship ("EBR"). If a funeral home has an EBR with a consumer, the funeral home may call the consumer even if the consumer's phone number is on the Do-Not-Call List. An EBR exists if (i) the funeral home has sold goods or services or entered into a financial transaction with the consumer in the eighteen months preceding the telephone solicitation; or (ii) in the three months preceding the telephone solicitation, the consumer inquired about goods or services offered by the funeral home and the relationship was not terminated by either party. If either of these two situations exists, the funeral home may contact the consumer.

It is important to note that the EBR exemption is limited only to the consumer with which the business relationship was established. For example, a funeral home that entered into an at-need contract with a widow to provide funeral services for her deceased husband could not rely upon the EBR exemption to solicit the children of the decedent. The funeral home could contact the widow, but no other family members unless they were also parties to the funeral contract.

Funeral homes that do engage in telemarketing should be aware of the other requirements of the telemarketing sales rules. There are provisions which restrict the time that calls may be made, requirements regarding mandating prompt identification of the telemarketer, the company they represent, and the purpose of the call, prohibitions against blocking caller ID, and other restrictions against abusive practices.

16.5 Fair Debt Collection Practices Act

The Fair Debt Collections Practices Act (the "FDCPA") was enacted to eliminate abusive practices in the collection of consumer debts. When a debt collectors is attempting to collect an obligation owed by a consumer, they are prohibited from taking any of the following actions:

- Contacting a consumer by telephone before 8:00 a.m. or after 9:00 p.m. local time.
- Not ceasing any further communication with a consumer once requested by the consumer.
- Calling the consumer numerous times with the intent to annoy, abuse or harass the consumer.
- Communicating with a consumer at his or her place of employment.
- Contacting the consumer when the consumer is represented by an attorney.
- Publishing the consumer's name and address on a bad debt list.
- Threatening arrest or legal action that is not permitted or demanding amounts that are not collectible under applicable law.
- Engaging in abusive or profane language.
- Reporting false information on the consumer's credit report.

In addition to the prohibitions noted above, the FDCPA requires a debt collectors to identify themselves, notify the consumer about the debt that is being collected, provide verification of the debt upon request, and notify the consumer of his or her right to dispute the debt.

Fortunately for funeral homes, the FDCPA does not apply to businesses seeking to collect their own debts. Therefore, the prohibitions and requirements of the FDCPA would not apply to a funeral home which is contacting consumers about overdue accounts and unpaid bills. It would, however, apply to any debt collectors or attorneys retained by the funeral home to collect a consumer debt. In addition, funeral homes should note that certain states, such as California, have their own laws which are very similar to the FDCPA and which regulate businesses trying to collect their own debts.